Who Is
Amy Schneider?

Who Is
Amy Schneider?

Questions on Growing Up, Being Curious, and Winning It Big on Jeopardy!

A Young Readers Edition of In the Form of a Question

AMY SCHNEIDER
With Tanya Lee Stone

Simon & Schuster Books for Young Readers

NEW YORK   AMSTERDAM/ANTWERP   LONDON
TORONTO   SYDNEY   NEW DELHI

SIMON & SCHUSTER BOOKS FOR YOUNG READERS
An imprint of Simon & Schuster Children's Publishing Division
1230 Avenue of the Americas, New York, New York 10020
Some names and identifying characteristics have been changed.
Text © 2023, 2025 by Amy Schneider
This young readers edition is adapted from *In the Form of a Question* by
Amy Schneider, published by Avid Reader Press in 2023.
Jacket illustration © 2025 by Petra Braun
Jacket design by Sarah Creech
SIMON & SCHUSTER BOOKS FOR YOUNG READERS
and related marks are trademarks of Simon & Schuster, LLC.
For information about special discounts for bulk purchases, please contact
Simon & Schuster Special Sales at 1-866-506-1949 or business@simonandschuster.com.
The Simon & Schuster Speakers Bureau can bring authors to your live event. For
more information or to book an event, contact the Simon & Schuster Speakers
Bureau at 1-866-248-3049 or visit our website at www.simonspeakers.com.
Interior design by Hilary Zarycky
The text for this book was set in Electra.
Manufactured in the United States of America
0125 BVG
First Edition
2 4 6 8 10 9 7 5 3 1
CIP data for this book is available from the Library of Congress.
ISBN 9781665933056
ISBN 9781665933070 (ebook)

To my mom, my first and best teacher

Contents

Author's Note

One of the best things about becoming well-known from *Jeopardy!* is all the young fans I have heard from. This book is for you! As you likely already know from the cover and the title page, my name is Amy. But what you might not know is that, until I was in my thirties, I went by a different name, the name my parents had given me. I was raised as a boy. Some part of me always knew that I wasn't a boy, but it took me a long time to figure that out. So now I go by Amy, and the personal pronouns I use are she/her. If you don't already know the term "transgender," a transgender person is someone whose gender identity is different from the one it was thought to be at birth.

This book is entirely my own story. Of course, many other people appear in this book besides myself. In some cases, I have changed names and details. Also, I want to be clear that I am describing people and events the way that I remember them, but I know that other people probably remember them differently than I do. So while I have tried to be as accurate and honest as possible, please keep in mind that this story is only being told from my point of view.

One of the key points I want to make in this book is that I am open to reconsidering my mindset. It is my hope that, in the future, I will come to disagree with some of the statements I've made in these pages, because it is my hope that I will never stop learning. I look forward to your feedback. The next book will be better.

CHAPTER ONE

What Is *Jeopardy!*?

"Did you always love Jeopardy!?"
"Did you win a lot of money?"
"Are you famous?"

F irst things first. Some of you may be wondering, *What is* Jeopardy! *anyway—and why am I about to read a book about one of its top contestants? What exactly is all the fuss about?* Well, let me give you a bit of an introduction to the game show that landed me in the national media spotlight and a brief history, so you can see for yourself how cool this quiz show is, and why, today, a lot of people know my name.

Jeopardy! first aired on TV way back in March 1964. This quiz show is unique because of its hook. Unlike the usual format of a quiz show, in which a host asks questions and contestants provide answers, *Jeopardy!* reverses that model. Contestants are shown the *answer*, and to win, they have to provide the *question*. For example, if a contestant chooses a square on the game board in a category called "Breakfast Cereals," the *Jeopardy!* host would read the spot on the board with a clue that might say, "The mascot of this cereal lives on the SS *Guppy*." And the correct answer would be "Who is Cap'n Crunch?" That's why I named the adult edition of this book *In the Form of a Question*.

Each game has three contestants who compete through three rounds—*Jeopardy!*, Double *Jeopardy!*, and Final *Jeopardy!*. During the *Jeopardy!* and Double *Jeopardy!* rounds, six categories with five clues each, worth different amounts of money, are shown on a big board, and as the dollar value gets higher, the clues get increasingly difficult. When a clue is selected, the first person to hit their buzzer gets the first shot at providing the solution (so you have to be fast as well as knowledgeable—more on that on page 15). If they're correct, they get the money from that clue, and they get to pick which clue is revealed next. For the *Jeopardy!* round, the winner of the previous game chooses both the category and the level.

For the Double *Jeopardy!* round, the contestant with the lowest score picks first.

KIDS' TV	SCIENCE	LET'S EAT	NARNIA	MEASURE IT	HOLIDAYS
$200	$200	$200	$200	$200	$200
$400	$400	$400	$400	$400	$400
$600	$600	$600	$600	$600	$600
$800	$800	$800	$800	$800	$800
$1000	$1000	$1000	$1000	$1000	$1000

A typical *Jeopardy!* game board.

The Final *Jeopardy!* round operates a bit differently from the first two rounds. Any contestant with zero dollars at the end of Double *Jeopardy!* is eliminated from the game, and Final *Jeopardy!* only has a single clue. The host announces the category before the round begins, which gives contestants a moment to consider how much they might know about it, and decide how much of their winnings they will choose to wager on their answer. Then the clue is revealed, and all the contestants write down their solution. If they get it right, they win the amount they wagered; otherwise they lose it. After all that, whoever has the most money is declared the winner. That day's winner returns the next day as the champion. When contestants talk about their "runs," they are referring to how many games in a row they won, keeping their "champion" status intact!

My love of *Jeopardy!* began when I was a kid. I watched it with my parents. Back then, it was hosted by Alex Trebek (he hosted the show longer than anyone else—for thirty-five years!). For me, as for so many others, *Jeopardy!* has been in the background of my life for as long as I can remember—a calm, comforting routine: three contestants, sixty-one clues, three Daily Doubles. Every weeknight, month after month, year after year. It was a place that valued the same things I'd been taught to value: curiosity, collegiality, rule following, and, above all, a sense that knowledge was fun! I always believed that I would compete on the show someday. While I didn't know what would happen once I did, I knew I wouldn't regret finding out.

I first auditioned for the show in 2008. As I recall, *Jeopardy!* had only recently begun offering their "entrance exam" online. It consisted of a timed test that had fifty questions, with fifteen seconds to answer each question. I was so excited. I crammed for a few days before, and (I'll admit) the first time, I kept a few tabs open in my browser with some things I might be able to check within fifteen seconds (Oscar winners, that sort of thing). I took the test every year for almost ten years. A few times I made it as far as the final, in-person audition. Then, for the next eighteen months, I'd live in hope that I would get the call to say I was in. When the call didn't come, I'd start the process over from the beginning.

I wasn't frustrated, because I knew that it was a numbers game and way more people qualify every year than can be on the show, so I just always told myself the longer it takes for me to get on, the more I'll have learned, and the better I'll do!

In 2017, I took a break from my *Jeopardy!* dream. A few years later, I decided to give it another go. One more time, I made it all the way to the in-person audition (although this time it was on Zoom). And then, again, I waited. It paid off. I got the call! In September 2021, I boarded a plane in Oakland, California, and flew to Los Angeles to be a contestant. I was going to be on *Jeopardy!*

I did well on the show. Really well! If I hadn't, I probably wouldn't be writing this book about my experience. Not that I wasn't ever nervous. Especially flying down there for my first taping when I realized that, whatever happened, I would never again have the possibility of a *Jeopardy!* experience to look forward to. That actually stressed me out, because I had spent my whole life waiting for this moment. I also knew that there was so much luck involved (remember the buzzer?) that the most likely outcome was going to be me playing one game and coming in second or third, and then it would all be over. So I told myself that I needed to go down there with a mindset of simply enjoying the experience. I was going to have fun, and the outcome would be whatever it was.

Have you ever been in a situation like that? All I had been thinking about was the possibility of losing and how upset I would be. And I just sort of realized that being afraid would be a terrible way to spend this day I'd been dreaming about. Of course, I still had some anxiety that day (and others), but I practiced telling myself to just stay in the moment and let those anxious thoughts go whenever they came into my head.

So . . . I played from November 2021 to January 2022,

and then I got to play again during the Tournament of Champions in November 2022. And here's an interesting fact: the only person who ever won more games than I did was *Jeopardy!* legend Ken Jennings when he was on the show in 2004—and he was the host when I was a contestant!

Here are a few of my stats:

- Won forty games in a row
- Second-longest winning streak in *Jeopardy!* history
- Received more than one million dollars in prize money
- Top-ten highest-earning (seventh) game show contestant on *any* American game show in history
- Most successful woman contestant to ever compete on the show

Now, I'm not listing these to brag. And these stats don't capture what I *really* took away from my time on *Jeopardy!* But they certainly caught people's attention. And some of those people started asking me a question, one that I'd been asked many times before, especially back when I was in school. The question was "How did you get so smart?"

For the record, it was not a question I enjoyed being asked, but the more I've learned about what it takes to be considered smart, the more I have come to understand that "smart" isn't simply something people are born with. There isn't only one kind of smart. It's not just about knowing facts and retaining them. It's also about knowing what facts are important and being able to access them at the right times. I think there's a lot of intelligence involved in figuring out a social life and managing relationships, in really listening to what people are asking. For example, sensing when your friends are looking for encouragement or advice, or whether or not they are just asking you to listen. That is an important type of intelligence. Knowing your own strengths and weaknesses is also really important. In other words, "book smart" isn't the only kind of smart.

Stick around, and I'll tell you why—and what all of this has to do with *you*.

CHAPTER TWO

How Did You Get So Smart?

"Really, how did you get so smart?"
"Do you have a photographic memory or something?"
"Are you, like, some kind of genius?"

These are questions I've been asked all my life. When I was a kid, these questions often felt like they were asked with some jealousy or negativity behind them. One reason for that was the environment I was raised in. I grew up in a large German Catholic community. Pride can mean many different things, but in Catholicism, pride is often seen as one of the worst sins, and in *my* Catholic community, taking too much pride in something, or being extremely talented at something, was bound to draw the wrong kind of attention—both from adults and from kids.

The negative attention I got from other kids was because, let's face it, kids can be bullies sometimes. But you know what? Being a kid can also be kind of scary. There comes a time when we start to realize that most grown-ups are really there to teach us how to do things for ourselves. They're training us in *being* a grown-up and being in charge of our own success. That is not a small deal. When some of my peers saw me succeeding more or less effortlessly at schoolwork, while they were barely getting by working their hardest, it likely scared them. Unfortunately for me, they showed that fear by putting me down. That meant that, from my point of view, every time I did something impressive, like winning five spelling bees in a row, getting perfect scores on test after test, or even using an unfamiliar word in a sentence, they would not like me. I started to pick up on this behavior, even when they tried to hide that bitterness.

I've always been a pretty empathetic person. I can easily understand and connect with other people's feelings. But being sensitive to other people's feelings sometimes makes you forget that your own feelings are important too. I started to put limits on my own abilities so I wouldn't seem so threatening. I discovered that if I blew off homework and studying, I could bring my grades down to a level that didn't seem to bother people around me, which was pretty much a win-win for me! (It's not like I *loved* homework and studying.) When someone still asked me why or how I knew something they didn't, I would assume it was because they were feeling resentful, so I would try to deflect their question in whatever way I could in the moment to keep their question from turning into an attack.

Now, fast-forward to the adult me, when I was on *Jeopardy!* every weeknight. For months, I succeeded spectacularly at a quiz game that tests players' knowledge about pretty much any category of information the writers choose. Since it's been on national television for decades, it's common knowledge that contestants have to be, well, smart! (They have to have a lot of other skills as well, and I'll let you in on some of these things in a minute.) Unsurprisingly, this success prompted all kinds of people—close friends, casual friends, coworkers, neighbors, flight attendants, cashiers at grocery stores, etc.— to ask me those same old questions from my childhood: "How did you get so smart? How do you know all that?"

I still didn't have a great answer. Even now, I am

sometimes tempted to reply, "How does anyone know anything?" But that response is unlikely to move the conversation forward, which is what I would prefer. I think intelligence is a really interesting thing to talk about, but I get uncomfortable talking about *my* intelligence. Due to my upbringing, I obviously can't just let somebody compliment me without resistance. If I went around letting people praise me willy-nilly, what would be next? Having self-worth? Pursuing my dreams? (Sarcasm alert! Of course you should have self-worth and pursue your dreams!)

To avoid such dire outcomes, I always use one of two general approaches.

One is to make the point that my intelligence is really due to factors outside my control. With this approach, I'll say that I was born with a brain that, for whatever reason, remembers knowledge well. (I don't have a "photographic" memory; the amount of time I've spent looking for my phone would disprove that.) For example, while many people who learn that the word "oviparous" means "egg-laying" will quite sensibly forget it almost immediately, I will probably remember it without any particular effort. I've never trained my memory or anything like that. No, I simply got a lucky roll of the genetic dice; in other words, I was born this way.

Another factor, of course, is the privilege I was born into. I never went a day without food or a night without shelter; I've never lived in a country that has been invaded. I had parents who were knowledgeable themselves, and who believed in the value of knowledge as its own reward. They nurtured my curiosity, and they were always willing to talk about things I was interested in. Moreover, I am white, and until well into adulthood, I was perceived as male. Had I been perceived as female growing up, I very likely would not have received the encouragement I did. Why, you may ask? Because our nation (and most nations) has had a long history of supporting boys' education over girls' education, and even though things are much better than when I was growing up, we still have a long way to go.

Lucky for me, I was never discouraged from acquiring knowledge.

My other general approach to the "how are you so smart" question is to simply deny it. There are many types of intelligence, and the one I have is hardly the most useful. Honestly, for most of my life I would have happily traded the type of intelligence that can name all the battles of the Thirty Years' War for the type of smarts that would have allowed me to be able to tell whether or not someone *likes* me, likes me. My skills at managing time and money are terrible. Even in the category of what some may call "pure intelligence," I have plenty of shortcomings: I'm terrible at chess, and higher math is just as bewildering to me as to most people. Surprisingly, being on *Jeopardy!* has actually given me new ways to both understand and talk about different ways of being "smart," because being good at *Jeopardy!* requires different skills than just being smart.

Jeopardy!, like sports, is an attempt to measure a natural talent through a made-up competition—it's like any other game, with rules created by game makers. So, on *Jeopardy!*, you don't just need to "know stuff"—you also need to know the right kind of stuff based on their rules and game structure. During my run, *Jeopardy!* aired a tournament for college professors, who are essentially *professional* knowers of stuff, yet their collective *Jeopardy!* performance was not particularly impressive. By design, *Jeopardy!* rewards breadth of knowledge, not depth. That means contestants who know an enormous amount about a fewer number of things don't do as well as contestants who know a little bit about a *lot* of things. This game structure happens to reward the combination of knowledge and laziness that's been my unique specialty since childhood (again, I'm using sarcasm).

Buzzer timing is also critical for doing well on *Jeopardy!* For whatever reason, it turns out that I'm good at beating my opponents to the buzzer when we *all* know the answer, and that has made me successful in a way that a more knowledgeable person with worse buzzer timing might not have been. I will say, the buzzer can be tricky! The buzzer was the thing that the crew probably talked to the contestants the most about during taping days. They warn you about getting frustrated, because it can be hard to tell whether you're coming in too early or too late with the buzzer. Sometimes I would lose the rhythm, but I usually had a pretty good feel for it.

Similarly, not getting anxious about answering the questions is also a factor in doing well. If I was being too conscious about it, overthinking things, then I didn't have a chance. I needed to get my rational thinking out of the way. It's kind of like memorizing lines in a play. When you're onstage, you can't stop and think about what the next line is, but if you just trust that you know it and say it, the lines (and the answers) are simply there.

There's one other skill that *Jeopardy!* requires. *Jeopardy!*'s central gimmick involves forcing a weird kind of grammar on the way the clues are given. That means you often have to figure out the question before you can even begin to find the answer. For example, a clue might read something like "A land bridge called al Lisan separates this 'corpse-like' body of water into a southern basin and a northern basin." That can be confusing if, like me, you've never heard of "al Lisan." But that's just camouflage! The clue actually comes down to the five words in the middle: "'corpse-like' body of water." What body of water could be called *corpse*-like? The *Dead* Sea!

Cutting through vague and sometimes confusing language in order to recognize the real question is the *Jeopardy!* skill that's most useful in daily life. It's ironic that while I was great at it as a contestant on the game, which won me money on TV, I was failing to apply it to real life.

You see, when a person asks me "How did you get so smart?" I still sometimes hear it in the same way I did when I was a child, which was "What, you think you're better than me?" But the reality is, that's not usually why people ask me that question these days. Mostly, what people are really asking is "How can *I* get smarter?" If that's at the heart of their question, the old answers I've been in the habit of giving are not just wrong; they could come across as a little rude or angry. If I tell you "I'm just lucky," that implies you can never be as smart as I am, since you weren't born with my gifts. And if I tell you "I'm not really that smart," that implies that you're not seeing things clearly, that the intelligence you say I have, or aspire to have for yourself, doesn't even exist.

Deep down, I don't even believe myself anymore when I offer those playful responses. They're true in their way, but they're hardly the entire truth. The fact is, I *do* know how I got so smart, and what it took. The real answer to "How did you get so smart?" is simply this: I wanted to. And if you want to, you can too!

Here's a perfect example: one response I gave on *Jeopardy!*, which my friends found supremely impressive, required knowing the meaning of that word I mentioned earlier, "oviparous." How could I know such a random fact? Well, if that definition *was* just a random bare fact, on its own, then it wouldn't have interested me, and I probably wouldn't have remembered it. But in reality, there are no "bare" facts. Everything is a thread in the infinite blanket of possible knowledge, and I want to explore as much of that blanket as I can.

I love that I will never, ever run out of things to learn. So, the way I see it, "oviparous" is not just an adjective for animals that lay eggs. Because I know that "ovi-" means "eggs," I can guess that "-parous" might mean something like "giving birth." And then, aha! I remember that an old-fashioned word for giving birth is "parturition," which means that "par-" is probably the same root. Now I have two weird vocabulary words connected in my mind, and I am much more likely to be able to recall each of them.

And it goes beyond that: wherever I first saw the word "oviparous," it was probably in an academic setting— perhaps in a science paper or article in the news. This reminds me that scientists tend to use fancy, scientific words like "oviparous" over more straightforward words, such as "egg-laying." Why do they do that? Well, it's partly because scientists need to be very precise, and using specialized words helps them communicate clearly with other scientists. But it's also because scientists are proud of themselves; they like being scientists, and they like the feeling of using words that only make sense to other scientists. It's just like having a group of friends that have some silly joke that only the friend group understands — it makes them feel like part of a special club, and that's a nice feeling. So thinking about this weird word has also let me think about how people form communities together, how scientists see themselves, and how to understand what scientists are trying to say.

Following these kinds of threads is a richly rewarding experience that will make you not just better at *Jeopardy!* but better at life — better at understanding what is going on around you, and why. Learning for its own sake is important, and knowledge will get you different things. But you may not know immediately which things, so if you just lean into learning about things you're truly interested in, that will lead you to more things you find interesting.

In other words, learning is for you, not for other people. Even when you have an assignment for school, if there is an opportunity to pick the topic for yourself — for a writing assignment, let's say — be sure to choose something you are excited to spend time thinking about. Knowledge is a shield and a sword, a joy and a duty, and while you may never use it to win a bunch of games on

Jeopardy!, if you have the desire to both know things and understand how they are connected, you can grow more and more powerful every day. Nobody will be able to stop you!

Plus, it's just fun to say. "Oviparous." Very satisfying.

CHAPTER THREE

What Teachers Made a Difference to You?

"What makes a teacher great?"
"Can teachers be outside a classroom setting?"
"Why do you love theater so much?"

When I was a senior in high school, my mother taught a math class at the University of Dayton, the college I would attend a year later. Since she hadn't completed her PhD, she usually taught math for students who had to take it for a requirement, which often meant they generally didn't like math at all. One day she wasn't feeling well, and she sent me in to monitor an exam she was giving. She said it would be fine; all I had to do was sit there and make sure the students weren't cheating.

Now, my mom was a teacher my whole life, but for

some reason I never really pictured her in a classroom. So when I saw the exam questions she had prepared, I was startled. They were great! I don't really remember what the test instructions said, but they had character, some jokes, and a little encouragement. I thought, *Oh, she's fun!* I don't know why I was surprised. I had heard her talk about the stories she would tell in her class, or assignments she gave, and they all sounded like the type of teaching I enjoyed. The classroom brought out the best in her.

And, of course, she'd always been a good teacher to me at home. One of the earliest such times I can remember was when she did an experiment with me. She had two different water glasses, one of which was empty. The empty one was tall and skinny. She poured the water from the shorter, wider glass into the tall, skinny glass, and then asked me if the second glass had more water than the first one. I said yes, clearly it did, because the water reached much higher in the skinny glass. She then tried to explain to me that it must be the same amount of water, since I had seen her pour it from one glass to the other, but I was still too young to get that. It always stuck with me, I think, because not only was she teaching me, she was showing me that she never stopped learning herself. In this case, she ran this experiment for herself. She wanted to understand how children learn about conservation.

Her modeling her own curiosity helped me understand that part of being a great teacher is having a sincere, contagious interest in the things you're teaching. When you are lucky enough to come across teachers like that, who are excited about learning, they can make a huge impact on your life. It might be by getting you excited about learning, or helping you understand more about who you are as a person, or simply seeing what your strengths are and encouraging you to pursue them.

Teachers are, potentially, everywhere in your life—not only in the classroom. They may not even have the title of teacher, so keep your eyes peeled. My mom was the first great teacher that I had, despite never having me in her class. Other people who had a part in shaping the person I am today did include some of my classroom teachers, but teachers also came into my life in the form of a soccer coach, theater camp counselor, drama director, and more. Let me tell you about some of them.

In first grade, I had Mrs. Coleman, who was a legend at my school. She was known as a disciplinarian, but she wasn't, really. She was just a strong, determined person- ality who made it very clear at all times that she was in charge and we were doing things her way, and that was the end of the discussion. When we were out in the world, on field trips or wherever, she'd carry a bell, and when she rang that bell, we would immediately stop whatever we were doing and line up behind her.

She was also the only Black teacher I ever had, in all my years of schooling. Mrs. Coleman was passionate about Black history, and she really impressed upon us the importance of learning some of that history. Martin Luther King Day was the biggest day on the first-grade calendar, with a pageant that we spent more time on, and were more excited about, than the Christmas pag- eant the month before. Her classroom had posters lined along the top of all four walls, each with a picture and short bio of a different Black activist or pioneer. There was Martin Luther King Jr., Rosa Parks, Phillis Wheatley, James McCune Smith, and many others. Mrs. Coleman brought Black heroes to our attention, people who did great things and were role models. Years later, my mother remembered a conversation she had heard me having with my best friend at the time, Elizabeth Jentleson, about how much we liked having her as a teacher.

From fourth through eighth grade, I had Mr. Reitz for at least one class each year. Mr. Reitz was there to help us through all our drama, especially in middle school. He was the only male teacher at the school, but he was also the most sensitive, and the best at resolving conflicts. When a particular bully was getting out of hand, or when a disputed call in a kickball game at recess had escalated to the point of a girl named Shawna sitting on home plate with the ball, crying while the class stood there yelling at her (full disclosure: I was no less guilty than the rest of the class in that moment), Mr. Reitz would call a "circle meeting." We would form our desks into a circle, Mr. Reitz included, and talk out whatever the issue was, using "I" statements, like "I (Shawna) feel sad when you yell at me, because I am doing my best."

He loved teaching, and not just about whatever the subject was at hand. He subscribed to the *New York Times*, and every Tuesday he would read the Science section and come in excited to share some new research with us. He had extra little facts for everything we were studying; the one that sticks out in my mind was about how the guns in the Old West were incredibly inaccurate, and you could shoot at someone and end up hitting someone else way off to the side. Many of his fun facts were exaggerated or misremembered, which is maybe not the *best* quality in a teacher, but the important thing was the excitement, the genuine joy he had in being able to share something with us that we didn't know.

On the last day of eighth grade, he asked us how we wanted to spend our final hour together, and somebody raised their hand and said, "Can we have a circle meeting?" And for one last time, we got our desks in a circle, and we all went around saying how much we'd meant to one another, and how much we'd miss those of us who weren't going to the same high school. It's a pretty great teacher who can get eighth graders to open up to one another like that!

During my freshman year of high school, Ms. Blier was my religion teacher. She was also the first teacher I ever had a crush on! She was fun and cool and bohemian, and she let us have class outside sometimes. She was the first liberal Catholic I'd ever encountered, and I was fascinated. Freshman year we studied the Old Testament, and she taught us to look at some of the stories from the female point of view instead of the male voice that is assumed, and the more traditional way to read them. I particularly remember her portrayal of Samson as a big dumb idiot, with Delilah as the long-suffering girlfriend exasperatedly keeping him out of trouble. Ms. Blier showed me that a text could be interpreted in different ways, and that when you are being taught something, you don't just have to choose between accepting or rejecting it; you can also choose to make it your own, no matter how authoritative the source claims to be.

I think she liked me, too; certainly I used all the grown-up-pleasing skills I had on her, and we had some good banter over the course of the year. She got engaged in the spring and brought her fiancé in to meet the class. He told us all to treat her well so that he wouldn't have to deal with her being grumpy when she got home. I then raised my hand and told him that he should treat her well for the same reason, and he turned to her and said, "Oh, this must be that Schneider kid you're always telling me about." I was clearly flustered, and after he left the room, Ms. Blier laughingly pointed out that the textbook on my desk had my name printed on it in big letters, which is why he called me out. I was proud to be teased as if I were a peer and not a student, but I must admit I was a little disappointed that she didn't actually talk about me all the time!

I also had two science teachers in high school who made a big impact. Ms. Anderson was my biology teacher, and I'm so glad that she was. Biology was one subject I never enjoyed. So much of what it dealt with was icky and gross, in my opinion. My standard line was "If God wanted us to know what our insides looked like, he would have given us tiny windows." And while I can't say I grew to love biology, I wasn't miserable, either, and Ms. Anderson was the reason why. It simply came down to the fact that she loved biology passionately, and the joy she got from it was infectious.

Mr. Korzan taught me chemistry and physics and seemed to have a great time doing it. He was consistently one of the least prepared teachers I'd ever had, but he made it work. In the very first week I had him as a chemistry teacher, he had us all do an experiment to combine Chemical A with something—water, baking soda, I don't remember—to turn it into Chemical B. (That's literally what he called them. He cared less about the specific chemical reactions involved at that point and more about getting us familiar with doing things in the lab.)

Only afterward, he found out that Chemical B was hazardous and couldn't be thrown away or washed down the sink, and needed some kind of special disposal. The entire rest of the school year, there was a tray in the corner of the lab filled with beakers of Chemical B. I never did find out what Chemical B was, or whether he ever figured out how to get rid of it or just left it there over the summer and hoped someone else would figure it out. It wouldn't have been out of character if he had.

He always wrote our tests at the very last minute, often in the car on his way into school that morning. So when we were taking the test, he'd be taking it himself, at his desk, and would occasionally say things like "Hey, everyone, on question four, that's supposed to be meters per second, not miles per hour," or "Hey, everyone, just skip question eight, it's not actually solvable the way I wrote it."

He also made us into characters in his word problems, and if you'd been annoying him, you could expect a question on the next test to say something like *Matt is riding his skateboard at 5 meters per second when he suddenly rolls off the edge of a cliff that's 200 meters tall. How far does he travel horizontally before smashing into the ground, and how fast is he going at the moment of impact?* (It was usually Matt, to be honest!) Making learning fun isn't a simple task, but Mr. Korzan made it seem easy. For better or worse, he's one of my role models for doing things at the last minute, and getting away with it!

And then there was Mr. Brooks. The best teacher I ever had. He taught me English freshman year, creative writing in at least one other year, and European authors my senior year. He was tall and thin, with bags under his eyes. I would joke that he looked like the ghost of Jacob Marley. He was extremely funny, but completely deadpan. Some of his lessons were legendary; the day he would teach prepositions, he would act them out, climbing up on his desk for "over," crouching beneath the tall chair he sometimes taught from for "under," and crawling out the other side for "through," things like that.

He oversaw the annual publication of *In Our Minds,* a collection of art and writing produced by students. When it came out, he would go around the classrooms trying to get people to buy it. Part of his sales pitch was "You should buy one before we run out. They're going like hotcakes. And you know how hotcakes go. Fast." I know it doesn't seem that way on the page, but I swear, when uttered with his deadpan delivery and pitch-perfect timing, it was one of the funniest things I've ever heard.

As a writing teacher, he wanted us to be familiar with a wide array of forms and styles, and he always supported us in whatever direction we wanted to go with our work. Senior year I'd discovered Kurt Vonnegut and gotten super into his work, so for my next assignment I turned in an essay that was an obvious imitation of the Vonnegut book *Hocus Pocus*. I filled it with short paragraphs, frequently jumping from one topic to something seemingly unrelated, talking directly to the reader, using everyday language. It wasn't the assignment, but he didn't mind. He saw how much I'd enjoyed it, how much fun I'd had with it, and that was all he wanted.

When I got to college, there was really only one teacher who stood out to me—but it wasn't for a reason you might expect. He taught me one of the only things I took away from college, which was "There are no win-win scenarios in computer science," an insight that applies to most things in life, I've found. He also did something I've always appreciated, which is that when I was about to graduate, he refused to write me a recommendation letter for prospective employers. He said to me, "Look, you're smart, you know the material, but you never did your homework, and in a workplace, you have to actually do the tasks you're assigned."

You might think I'd have been resentful, but in fact I felt nothing but respect. I knew perfectly well that I was a slacker, that I made a habit of counting on my natural abilities to avoid any serious consequences. I felt bad about it, and I regretted the opportunities I could have had if I'd worked harder, if I'd maximized my abilities. I resented all the people in my life who had so consistently allowed me to get away with it. It was nice that, in the final days of my academic career, someone finally told me that they saw me, they understood what I was doing, and they were disappointed that I wasn't doing better than "good enough."

But remember, as I said earlier, some of my greatest teachers didn't teach me in a traditional classroom. There was a soccer coach in eighth grade who motivated me to actually exercise regularly, including outside of soccer practice, which is a gift I've only grown to value more as I've gotten older. And the leader of our church youth choir, whose love of music, and belief in us, was so powerful that we found ourselves singing quite beautifully without knowing how we did it. But the ones I remember the most were all from the theater experiences I had growing up—and three of them shaped my life profoundly.

Jean Howat Berry ran the summer youth theater camps at the Dayton Playhouse. Ms. Berry took it very seriously and tried to get us to understand what made it more than "playing pretend." I had recently been in my first play, because my cousin's college production of *The Music Man* needed town kids, and it was a lot of fun. (Any time I got to hang out with grown-ups was fun for me.)

Then that summer at camp, Ms. Berry walked up to me one day and said, "Come on, I want you to sing for these people," and next thing I knew I'd been cast in an adult community theater production of *Mame* as Young Patrick, a fairly important role. If you were a kid willing to do theater, Ms. Berry would give you every opportunity she could. I learned a little of everything: how to light a stage, how to run sound, how to dress a set, how to call a show as a stage manager. No part of the playhouse was off limits to us kids when we were with her. And she produced some great shows along the way.

Another inspiring teacher I had was Lisa Howard-Welch. She taught me that there was nothing wrong with attempting the impossible. It was highly unlikely that a youth theater company focused on Shakespeare and Jane Austen would really work, but she tried anyway. Because whether or not grandiose dreams can succeed, it's worthwhile to model reaching for those dreams no matter what. W. Shakespeare & Co. may have been a wild idea, but I will forever be grateful that she had it. She also really empowered us to take ownership of the process. We all had to pitch in and help build the sets. During *The Tempest*, she asked me and my cousin/friend Jacob to make this functioning hourglass prop for the character of Prospero. There were no instructions, so we figured it out, using plastic liter bottles and aquarium gravel. It was a great feeling that she trusted us to solve the problem and get the job done!

In high school, I was part of the Drama Club, and Ms. Fran Pesch was in charge. I personally considered Drama Club to be a required class, never mind the fact that it took place outside of school hours and nobody received grades. Some people teaching theater are great because they are focused on empowering the kids to be their best. Not Ms. Pesch. Ms. Pesch was great because she was focused on the *theater*. She was there to put on the best show she could, and the fact that we were children was just one more obstacle she had to overcome. (Producing pretty much any kind of theatrical production consists entirely of navigating an infinite series of obstacles. It's like playing Super Mario Bros., except that all the mushrooms and turtles are real people who you might need to work with in the future.)

Ms. Pesch was an advocate for the audience, not for the cast. She understood that when the Drama Club put on one of their handful of shows each year, nearly everyone in the audience *had* to be there. They had a friend or relative in the cast, and they didn't have a choice as to whether or not they would attend. She wanted the performances to be great for *them*.

Her notes always emphasized keeping the show moving, not leaving any dead air. "Pace, pace, pace!" she would say. And she was always moving herself—she never dragged, never held back, never dawdled. When she was directing, whether she was blocking out a scene in rehearsal, or making a general announcement about scheduling, or running an audition, she was never, ever boring.

And she was also never, ever hurtful. All of the above

might make her sound like a bit of a tyrant, but she wasn't. She never asked us to do things we weren't capable of, but she wouldn't let us do less than we were capable of either. Not because we owed it to her, or to ourselves, but because we owed it to the audience. She taught me that the work you do doesn't matter unless it is being done in the service of others, and that doing just okay isn't enough. You can't feel satisfied unless you know you did your best. Not *the* best, just the best you had in you each day.

So that's the thread running through all these memories, connecting all the good teachers (including some I haven't mentioned here—I'm grateful to you as well!) who came into my life. As you've seen, a great teacher doesn't just teach their material—they advocate for it. They show you not just what you should know, but why you should care about it, often simply by showing the pleasure they take from knowing it themselves. I'm lucky to have had so many teachers do that for me, and my hope is that I can do the same for you. I hope I'm able to show people the joy I take in learning, in knowledge. If I succeed in that, it's all thanks to the names in this chapter, and I'd be honored to have passed on the gift that they've given to me.

Sometimes, especially when you are younger, your teachers are assigned to you, and you get really lucky. As you get older, there will likely be more opportunities to choose your teachers and what things you want to be taught. Along with your classes, you'll get to try out extracurricular activities, like theater or soccer. That's one reason it's good to appreciate your teachers and what they bring to your life — so you can keep finding the ones that fit with you.

Like teachers, the people you call your friends also have the power to make a huge difference in your life. Choose them wisely as well, and you will have a lot to be thankful for, just like me.

CHAPTER FOUR

What Makes a Good Friend?

"Where are you from?"
"Who was your best friend growing up?"
"What does feeling at home have to do with friends?"

W here are you from?"

It's one of the classic small-talk questions, and I have part of my answer down pat:

"I live in Oakland, by Lake Merritt, near Fairyland. I was born and raised in Dayton, Ohio, but I've been in Oakland since 2009, and I don't ever plan to leave. It's home." Then, if I'm asked about Dayton specifically, my usual line is "It's a great place to be *from*," with both the insult and the compliment intended. I do love Dayton, and I don't regret my time there. But I'm glad I don't live there anymore.

People sometimes ask *why* Oakland is home to me while Dayton is not, and I always find it hard to explain. Let me try a new way. It has a lot to do with friendship.

When I was growing up in Dayton, my cousin Jacob was my best friend. Some of my favorite memories are of things we worked on together. We both loved the Redwall books, and sometime during fourth or fifth grade, we spent a long time working on a Redwall story of our own. Although it wasn't actually set in Redwall, it did have animal characters that went on epic adventures, and cool swords and silly jokes and scary villains. It was so much fun to make something that had ideas from both of us in it.

I also remember when we were asked to make a banner for a school mass. I don't remember what message we chose to put on the banner, but I do remember going through all the fabrics with him and picking out a shiny silver for the image in the center. I loved getting to do the sort of hands-on craft work that boys didn't usually get to do—at least not the boys in our community back then. More importantly, Jacob made me feel at *home*.

Sixth grade, as far as friendships went, was the worst. But I learned something that has lasted a lifetime. The boys were mean to one another; there were a dozen or so of us in the class, and each of us knew exactly where we ranked in the popularity order (it was confirmed every day when we picked teams for kickball at recess), and we were constantly struggling not to lose our spot. The worst part of it was, the boys closest to you in the order were the very ones you'd been friends with, and now they were suddenly your competition. I remember one good friend, just slightly more popular than I was, suddenly wouldn't hang out with me anymore. And I remember how much that hurt. I also remember that I did the same thing to those below me, even making fun of Jacob sometimes just to make sure I stayed above him. But when I saw how hurt he was when I did that, I realized I didn't want to be a mean person, and I knew that I should only be friends with people who treated me like friends. If that was going to make me "less popular," then . . . so what? Anyone who was hurtful wasn't somebody I wanted to be popular with anyway.

Apart from early childhood, the first time I really felt at home was my senior year of high school. It didn't have anything to do with where I lived (trust me—I slept in the top bunk of a bunk bed, crammed in a closet-sized bedroom only slightly bigger than the bed itself, in an old house in an old neighborhood); it had to do with who I hung out with. I had friends who I was close to. I knew my place in the social scene. I had a driver's license. I was having new experiences all the time. It was the best time of my life so far, and I knew it. I would say to myself, *This is it. This is the good life; this is my peak. College won't be like this, and probably not adult life either. I'm not going to get this back, and I need to enjoy it now.*

Here's a random example, and I know it might not sound as great as it felt: One day my friends Ben and Beth picked me up from a *Twelfth Night* rehearsal. They told me that we were going to see a movie I liked, but when we got there, they told me we were really going to see a different movie, one that I'd already told them I didn't want to see. But they wanted me to see it, so they dragged me along, knowing that I actually liked being tricked into spending time with them, even if I didn't know it. And so, even though I didn't actually like the movie itself, it's still one of my happiest memories.

I loved that I had a role in their lives and a place in our friend group, that I was the one who they wanted with them. They tricked me into seeing the movie because they thought that I would like it, but also because they just wanted me to be there with them. It was the most accepted I had felt in my life, and I knew it was about to disappear.

And it did. Beth went off to art school in New York, because she's one of the coolest human beings I've ever met. Ben went off to school in Toledo—not quite as cool, but at least he went somewhere out of town. I stayed in Dayton. If I'd worked harder in school or if my family had had more money, I'd have gone somewhere else. But I hadn't, and they didn't, and my dad worked at UD, so I got free tuition; so that's where I was. The University of Dayton, despite its many fine qualities, was perhaps the least homelike place I've ever been. Fraternities, which are male social clubs, ruled the campus—either you were part of them, or you weren't. I wasn't in a fraternity; I didn't even want to be in one, and I hated it there. I had to live in student housing the first two years, so I had to share my space with strangers, which was not fun. I swore a solemn oath to myself after sophomore year that I would never live with roommates ever again. Those dorms never felt like home; they were just beds assigned to me in a nightmarish summer camp that lasted for eight months.

The first place I lived on my own was a furnished one bedroom at the top of a hill near campus, and while I'd hoped it would feel like home, it never did. The place was big and empty except for random pieces of other people's furniture. The landlords lived across the street with their large family, several of whom always seemed to be hanging around the office whenever I went in to drop off my rent money, staring wordlessly at me until I left. I was afraid of them.

It was a pretty lonely existence. One day a fly got in. I spent a few days trying to kill it with a rolled-up newspaper, and it kept evading me. It got to where I almost respected the fly for being so good at surviving. Then I went to the store and got an actual flyswatter. It turns out there's a reason there's a specific design for flyswatters. The first time I took a swing at the fly with it, I killed it. And I was devastated. We'd had a whole relationship going, that fly and me! That poor fly never had a chance once I acquired flyswatting technology. So now it was just me again, sitting on a couch that didn't belong to me, that had never belonged to anyone, watching the room darken and feeling a creeping sense of dread.

Meanwhile, I kept getting glimpses of a world where I

could feel at home with people who could be my friends. I visited Beth at Cooper Union in New York, and while I was there, I went with her to a party with a bunch of art students. We got silly and happy and had absurd conversations that I knew I would think about for a long time afterward. A woman hauled out her acoustic guitar and sang "Both Hands" by Ani DiFranco. I was enthralled. I'd never seen that happen at a party at my school.

This is where I should be, I thought, looking around that room. These were people with whom I could discuss books and Taoism, people who were open to different ways of thinking about how to live, people who would drag me to movies because they wanted me around.

At the time, I didn't think I would ever get to be anywhere like that. But things change, and a few years later I had a wife, Kelly, and we were moving out of Ohio. Kelly and I had met in 2004, when we were both in a community theater production of *The Taming of the Shrew*. I was twenty-five, and she turned twenty-two twelve days after we met. We were raised in the same type of family, shared the same sense of humor, liked talking about our favorite bands, etc. We started dating and got married about a year and a half later. Kelly opened me up to so many things, but maybe the best of them was the idea that I could actually leave Ohio and make a new home somewhere else. At first, we went to California from Ohio to visit some friends of hers, but the more time we spent there, the more it struck both of us as our kind of place.

I had never thought that I would leave the Dayton area. Leaving seemed to be for other people. In my family, no one moved away. I had the feeling that living somewhere beautiful wasn't my fate. The fate of my family was to be in southwest Ohio, and that was that.

Plus, the idea of moving away may have been exciting, but it was also scary. I knew where everything was in Dayton. I knew how to get from anywhere to anywhere, and I didn't get lost, even though I didn't have a smartphone. I knew people there, although not that many. Most of my friends were Kelly's friends, and she had just graduated college, so a lot of them had moved to various places around the country, but there were still a few we hung out with. The thought of going somewhere so far away, and being apart from the few friends that I had, was definitely intimidating.

But Kelly made a convincing argument for trying something new, and we decided to move to California.

The whole time I kept not believing that we were doing it, even as we found an apartment and hired movers, packed up all our stuff. But when it sank in that we were actually moving, I realized that I didn't really think I was ever coming back. Even so, all our relatives on both sides believed we would return, and pretty quickly at that.

You'll miss the seasons! they said (I have never once missed the seasons, even a little), or *It's so expensive out there!* or *Isn't Oakland really dangerous?*

But what I heard was *Our kind of people don't go to California. You won't like it there. The people will be weird and different, and you'll want to come home to old familiar Ohio.*

I doubted it.

So we drove across the country to our new Oakland home.

If you want to know why Oakland is great, there's no substitute for just moving there. It worked for me. While I never seem to be able to explain why Oakland is the greatest city in the world, I can at least try to capture some of its appeal to me.

A few days after we first moved there, we went to a party a block from our new apartment with some of

Kelly's friends' friends. It reminded me of those parties in New York with Beth. Only now I wasn't a tourist just visiting for the weekend before going back to Dayton. I wasn't wishing I could belong this time, because I *did* belong at this party, with these people. I can't say what it was about them that I responded to specifically, and I'm not sure that I ever met any of them again after that night. All I remember, really, is that we had interesting conversations.

I didn't have to be careful of sounding too smart or saying things that they didn't understand. Because if I did use a word or a concept that they weren't familiar with, that wasn't a problem for them. In Ohio, it had always seemed like a problem. It felt like I had always gotten in trouble for saying something that was on my mind or for knowing stuff that made other people feel dumb. But from that night on, I was in Oakland, I belonged there, and that was kind of that.

I still feel that way. California has great weather, and the landscape is stunningly gorgeous. Every week I'm out here, I see something that would've been the most beautiful thing I'd ever seen back in Ohio. People in California leave their windows open all the time. Constantly being in the fresh air, indoors or out, was something I'd never considered in Ohio, where you needed either heat or air-conditioning for fifty-one weeks out of the year. At the farmers market there's always incredible produce, peaches and plums and strawberries, kale and peppers and potatoes. For a month or two each summer this one farm sells blueberries that are so amazing, they've ruined all other blueberries for me, not that I'm complaining.

I found my home and I found my friends. My hope is that you all have friends who make you feel at home too.

CHAPTER FIVE

When Did You Know You Were Trans?

"Were there clues?"
"Were you sure?"
"Who did you tell?"

For the first thirty years of my life, if you had asked me if I was a trans woman, I would have said no. Some people *had* asked me that, in fact, and I had denied it. Yet when I look back, the evidence was in front of me all along. Had I known this plot twist was coming the whole time? And if not, when did I know? I'm not sure. But I can see a lot of clues, times in my life when I might have known.

I might have known in third grade. You see, in second grade, I loved the American Girl books. Well, I say the American Girl books, but I would almost always just reread the Molly books. Yes, Samantha and Kirsten were fine, and they had that same quality of being part of a larger story, while still having relatable age-appropriate problems and stakes, but I was all about Molly McIntire.

Molly lives in the Midwest and her dad's off fighting in World War II, and she has her two girlfriends. (I only had one girlfriend, Elizabeth Jentleson, but she was a really good friend.) She tries hard to be well-behaved, but sometimes circumstances work against her, and she has this beautiful dress that she wants to wear for the patriotism pageant that the town is planning. She wears glasses and sweaters, and I thought she was pretty. I just liked her. She was kind of like the sassy Ramona Quimby character from the Beverly Cleary books I loved growing up, except that Molly was helping win World War II. I appreciated that she was born in the 1930s, making her about my grandmother's age. Close enough to my time to be familiar, distant enough to be mysterious.

While I liked the books, I didn't really play with the dolls that came with them. I had already learned that dolls were not for boys. Every Christmas, my mom would make a doll for each of my female cousins, in the traditional costume of different peoples each year. One year the costume would be from India, another year it might be from Nigeria or Sweden. Really, any country that my mom happened to be interested in. I even helped her make them, using a chopstick to shove the stuffing into the arms and legs she had sewn. I didn't think much about the fact that she only gave them to the girls in the family until I was older. I just remember thinking that dolls didn't much appeal to me.

I preferred my stuffed animals. Outdoors Bear, who my mom made because we couldn't afford a Care Bear, was my favorite. (He is still with me, right now, in fact, as I write this book.) There was also a rotating cast of supporting characters. But stuffed animals were for sleeping. Otherwise, when it came to toys that were supposed to have human qualities, I didn't see the point. I liked Transformers, or most of the He-Man toys, the ones that had parts you could play around with, like cycling Man-E-Faces through his multiple faces, or extending Mekaneck's . . . neck. (Look, I didn't name them.) Beyond that, I didn't get why I should pretend a toy was a person. When I wanted to think about other people's perspectives, I read books.

Apart from that, I'd gotten a glimpse at the price of an

American Girl doll at some point, and it was one of those numbers that I knew there was no point even discussing with my parents. So with all that, I didn't feel particularly deprived of the dolls. But neither did I feel that there was any reason not to read the books that came with them and feel the excitement every time as Molly once again nailed her audition to play Miss Victory. But one day, not long after we started third grade, a classmate saw me reading one of the books and said, "Those are for girls. Boys aren't supposed to read those."

"Oh! Okay!" I said, and I stopped reading them. Just like that. I deprived myself of a joy in my life, because it was a joy I was told only girls were allowed to feel. Life already seemed to be full of joys that one wasn't allowed to feel, so adding one more to the pile came pretty naturally. So yes, there were times I could have known. If I think back even earlier, there were other clues too.

I might have known as soon as I started being able to dress myself. Once I learned that some types of clothes were only permitted for girls, I didn't wear them, but you better believe I wanted to. I was so envious of girls, because they had so many more choices about how they looked. Boys could only wear a few types of clothes and only get one kind of haircut. I thought it would be amazing to have options! To be able to have your hair long or short, with bangs or without, and then whenever you wanted a change you could put it up into a bun or a ponytail or pigtails, or who even knows what! And all the different pretty clothes they could wear, are you kidding me? Don't even get me started on accessories! Or manicures! Though now that I can get manicures, I do struggle with them. I love having a pretty color on my nails, but keeping a manicure requires many skills I don't possess: Sitting still. Planning. Not constantly fidgeting.

I was grateful that the school at Corpus Christi Parish required a uniform. It was somewhat of a relief that I didn't have to choose the clothes I wore; the decision wasn't up to me. Deciding what to wear was always stressful for me. How could I decide, when every choice I had was ugly? All of it ill-fitting, too big, and cut for a different body. But I didn't see any alternative, any possible way of being happy with how I looked. My primary motivation in life back then was to be mocked as little as possible. I could never dress right; I could never be cool; I could never be pretty. So I mostly just tried to be invisible.

I could have known then that I wasn't a boy, given

the fact that I hated every article of boys' clothing that I had ever seen or even thought of, and I felt like I chose my outfits as part of an elaborate prank I was playing on myself. But I still didn't know.

When I look back, one of the clearest ways in which my true gender showed up in my childhood was my intense dislike of the Boy Scouts. Although "dislike" doesn't get it across. I hated it; I feared it; I found it disgusting and disturbing. I had enjoyed Cub Scouts, especially the Pinewood Derby, a wooden-car racing event that, typically, fathers and sons took part in together, making a little race car out of a block of wood. The goal was to race it against the cars the other kids had made by placing them at the top of a slanted board and allowing them to roll down to the finish line. There was some basic physics to it, which was also fun.

My dad didn't get to play the role of my teacher as often as my mom did, given that she was an actual teacher and also worked shorter hours, and thus had more time with me. But down in the basement workshop where we were making our car, we talked about things like how to reduce drag (in retrospect, probably a pretty small factor) or where to apply fishing weights to best distribute the mass of the car. The car had to be beneath a certain weight limit. In practice, this meant every car was exactly at the weight limit, or as near as possible. But there was also an artistic side to it. For instance, we had to choose what color to paint the car, and I'll always remember my dad telling me how British cars were painted "racing green," and our discussion of how we would set the fishing weights in the middle so it looked as if there were people in the car.

Granted, it didn't feel so fun when the day of the contest arrived and our car didn't win. I hope I didn't make it too obvious, but I blamed my dad. This felt like a class project, and I always won (or got the best grades on) class projects. It must be my dumb dad's fault! So yeah, that's one of my favorite memories of my dad, and it ends with me resenting him for something that wasn't remotely his fault. I'm sorry about how confusing it was for my dad to have me as a kid. He was given the job of making a man out of me, and he was doomed from the start. But none of us knew that yet.

Which is why he insisted I join the Boy Scouts. I don't even know if he insisted, really. Boy Scouts was just the thing that came next, part of the schedule of my childhood. At a certain age you started going to middle school, and you started going to Boy Scouts, and you started being awful to your peers.

Middle school is the worst, this period after you learn how excited and powerful you feel when you hurt someone else, but before you learn that you still shouldn't do that. At the end of the first meeting I went to with my Boy Scout troop, some of the boys started chasing this other guy around the parking lot to beat him up for some reason. Probably no reason.

I had no idea what was going on, and I got the impression that this was just how every Boy Scout meeting wrapped up. And if there were going to be chasers and chased, I knew which side I wanted to be on, so I joined in, but I was miserable. The main problem was that I hated boys. And Boy Scouts was nothing *but* boys! I was having a hard enough time at school; another disastrous aspect of middle school was that I wasn't allowed to hang out with girls on the playground anymore. But when I was at school, at least girls were *around*. Without their presence, boys were even more horrifying. Myself included.

I had nothing against our scoutmaster. He was a good

person doing his best, a veteran trying to instill good character in us in a wholesome way, passing down the values he'd learned. But he wanted to keep us boys busy, and by busy he didn't mean *thinking*.

Haven't you got something to do?

What are you doing sitting down?

Why are your hands in your pockets? Do something!

Where he really lost me was: *What are you doing reading a* book?, as if he couldn't imagine anything less productive. But all I wanted to do was read. I couldn't imagine how engaging with the real world could benefit me. It didn't seem to have done me any good so far.

So as the day approached when I would be going to Boy Scout camp, an entire week in the belly of the beast, I was filled with as much dread as I've experienced in my entire life. I hated the thought of Boy Scout camp. It felt like the last straw, the culmination of all the things I hated. Birthday parties, basketball, Little League, whatever, I was *always* being sent off to be with boys and do boy things, and I hated it. But there was no use in hating it. It wouldn't get me anywhere.

It was a real conundrum. My whole way of dealing with the discomfort I felt, the feeling that I was always somehow wrong, was to identify and follow all the rules so I could avoid being punished. But then one of the most important rules turned out to be that I had to hang out with boys all the time and do what they did, up to and including Boy Scout camp, which felt like the biggest punishment of all. And not only that—I was supposed to like it! As far as everybody else could see, Boy Scout camp was an *opportunity*. An opportunity to hang out with other boys, bond with my peers, learn valuable lessons about how to be the man I was doomed to become.

Sure, I could rebel, make a ruckus, get everybody all upset and angry at me, but I could have done that at any time. And then what? Everyone would be angry at me; my parents would withdraw their affection; my peers would mock me; people would think I wasn't smart, that I was a little kid, barred from the grown-ups' table. In short, I would be In Trouble, the worst possible state of being. And they'd still make me go to Boy Scout camp!

So I went. And you know, a funny thing happened: once I actually got there, accepted my fate, and began really participating . . . I hated it just as much as I'd thought I would! Possibly more! When I look back at my life from ages twelve to thirty, the image that always comes into my head is of those stories you read where a cop goes undercover in some evil organization for, like, ten years, and if they were ever discovered, they'd be doomed. That is what life as a boy was like for me, except there was no police department ready to evacuate me. That feeling was never stronger than during that week at Boy Scout camp.

The whole boy thing was just so exhausting, and I never felt like I got it quite right. I was always on the verge of being exposed as unmanly, and I had no idea how to avoid it. That I was not a boy was not a possibility I considered; I assumed that other boys felt the same, that they found it just as exhausting and unbearable. I thought they had somehow managed to put on a convincing show that they actually liked being boys, and I didn't know why it was so hard for me to do the same.

Since failing at boy-ness seemed to be an unforgivable sin, my only hope was to not be noticed. Each new encounter with another human being could be the one where I slipped up and had my cover blown, and was punished, possibly with violence. It was generally agreed that, even if you didn't approve of violence, effeminate boys were "just asking to get beat up," and bore at least some of the responsibility when it happened. So if it ever became obvious to the other boys how much I didn't belong, some unspecified but terrible punishment would surely be my fate. Boy Scout camp raised that experience to another level. It was like Indiana Jones in *The Last Crusade* when he's retrieving his dad's diary in Berlin, surrounded by nothing but Nazis as far as the eye can see.

I don't remember much of what happened that week through the fog of dread and despair that suffuses those memories. In the middle of the week, our parents came for an evening, and we had a ceremony of some kind. I barely said a word the whole time, although, to be fair, at this point in my life I rarely said anything to my parents. My mom would do her impression of me for her friends: "How was your day at school? 'Good.' What did you do? 'Nothing.' Really, nothing? 'I don't know.'" That sort of thing.

But that evening I was particularly mute. All I wanted was to burst into tears and say I wanted to go home. The next day, I got swimmer's ear, and they took me off-site to see the doctor. He diagnosed it, gave me some antibiotics and earplugs, and sent me back to camp, where I went to the one phone we could occasionally use, called my mom, and said, "I need to go home! The doctor said so!" The doctor had in no way said that. I'm pretty sure he explicitly said there was *no* need for me to go home. But I had already decided that this was my ticket out of there, and I wasn't going to give it up. The scoutmaster seemed disappointed, but relieved. He'd probably realized that I was not a problem he was going to be able to solve.

My mom came and picked me up, and as we were driving home, she said, "I came yesterday completely prepared to take you home. I thought that that was what you would want. And you didn't say anything."

I was glad to hear my mom admit that she knew I didn't like the Scouts; there'd been a kind of grim determination among all of us to insist that, actually, I was having a great time. But I also felt betrayed. *Of course I didn't say I hated Boy Scout camp! I wasn't supposed to say that! I was being good, and as a reward you drove away and left me there!*

A week later, the proof arrived that my scoutmaster had given up on me: my merit badges for the classes I'd started at camp, but not finished, came in the mail. It was a kindness. My scoutmaster knew that I had been told by my parents that I had to stay in Boy Scouts at least until

I made it to the rank of Second Class. Not a particularly challenging achievement, as the name implies, unless of course everything you're required to do makes you feel sick to your soul. My ticket to freedom was three merit badges: basketry, leatherworking, and swimming. The basketry and swimming I did at least kind of earn. I knew how to swim, and I'd woven a basket. But when it came to leatherworking, I hadn't done a single thing. It was simply a gift from my scoutmaster to me—he let me off the hook, and I was grateful.

But you know, everything in life is a learning experience. What did I learn from Boy Scouts? I *should* have learned the value of speaking up about my needs; if I had just told my mom how I felt that night, I would have been spared another day of agony, and my mom would have been spared a two-hour round trip. But I didn't.

No, when I think about it, looking back, there's only one lesson I learned, and even that one I didn't really fully grasp for decades afterward. The only thing I learned from being in the Boy Scouts was: I'm not a boy. Not even Second Class.

And I was about to face a much bigger dilemma. Puberty had arrived.

I don't mean to alarm you, but hitting puberty when you *already* hate your appearance is not the most pleasant experience. A lot of the changes that were taking place were ones that I'd been dreading for a while, primarily that I'd be growing hair seemingly everywhere, all sorts of places, places where I could not imagine any use for it. I mean, c'mon, my back? My back?! But what I hated most was hearing my voice change.

I'd been singing in the church choir and in musicals for years, and while I wasn't *that* good, I enjoyed it, and I knew I could at least carry a tune. I was an alto. I would stand with the other altos during rehearsals for the musical *Scrooge* or something, and we would chat with one another, about a tricky passage in the score, about the soprano who took every opportunity to show off her range (you know there's always one!), or about the unjust way in which altos never got the interesting parts, whatever.

My mom and I used to take part in a sing-along of Handel's oratorio *Messiah* every December. We would share a music book and sing in the alto section together, and I was at least better than she was, and there were so many people singing that you could sing as loud as you wanted and still feel anonymous. And maybe it felt good when some of the old ladies standing near you would say something to your mom between songs about how they enjoyed hearing her little boy singing out so strong.

But then my voice changed. That was it for singing. I assumed I still *could* sing, but I couldn't sing alto. What was I supposed to do? Sing tenor or baritone? Go stand over there, with all the boys? No thank you! I made an exception for musicals. The Drama Club was my friend group in high school, and they expected me there. But I couldn't enjoy them in the same way I used to. I could never imagine myself stealing the show with an incredible musical solo, as I had once or twice before. That might have clued me in that this whole "boy" thing was not for me. But it didn't. Singing became just another pleasure to toss on the trash pile with *Molly Saves the Day*.

I also might have figured it out in my other theater experiences. Although I'd been raised at home and by the church to think otherwise, theater taught me that it was okay to be a gay man. When I was about thirteen years old, I was in a production of *Oliver!* A group of us were waiting for our parents to pick us up: me, the boy playing Oliver, and one of the girls who was in the chorus with me.

For whatever reason, the subject of Elton John came

up in conversation. And the boy playing Oliver said something along the lines of "Oh, I don't like Elton John; he sings songs to his *boyfriend*." And the girl—who was a couple of years older than either of us, and taller and stronger—grabbed him by the collar and said, "This is *theater*. We don't *say* things like that." It was one of the coolest moments I've ever seen in person. It was from that moment on that I never really could get behind thinking that there was anything wrong with gay people, and it's the same sort of thing as with thinking about trans people.

It's easy to think that there's something wrong with it if that's what you are told when you're growing up. But once you stop and think about it, and ask yourself, *What is the problem, actually?*, you realize that there isn't one. I thought it was so interesting that it was just like flipping a switch, that thirty seconds before, I would have completely agreed with that boy thinking that Elton John was silly or gross, and then thirty seconds after, I didn't anymore—and that was that.

A couple of years later, I was cast as Algernon in *The Importance of Being Earnest*. I fell into that role with an eagerness that might as well have been a flashing neon sign saying AMY IS A WOMAN that I'm shocked I didn't see. Thanks to my "this is *theater*" experience, it didn't bother me that Algernon was a flamboyantly gay character.

The play is fun and challenging. Every line seems a hundred words long, and Algernon delivers many of them while eating cucumber sandwiches. But more of a gift than that: it was a chance for me to sway my hips the way I thought they should sway, to gesture with my hands when I talked, to end way more sentences on uptalk (which is when you finish every sentence as if it's a question), to hold a glass with the fewest fingers necessary. Not only was I allowed to violate practically every rule in the Boy Code—how you could walk, how you could move your hands while you were talking, what kinds of clothes you could wear and how you felt about them—I was actually *encouraged* to do so. And I was rewarded for it with the praise I craved.

I'll never forget being backstage before one of the shows. I was feeling some stage fright and worrying about my lines. And my cousin/best friend/castmate Jacob, who would come onstage a few minutes after me, saw me stressing out and calmed me down by saying, "Hey, okay, hold up. Take a breath. Now: let me see you do your

Algernon walk. You know that always makes you happy."

And he was right. I perked up, thrust my shoulders back, and sashayed my way back and forth a few times. Letting my body flow how it wanted, letting it show how it felt, that always made me happy. Would it have been nice to feel that happy in any other context than a poorly attended youth theater production of an Oscar Wilde play? Sure! But that was the only context that I'd ever heard of, or really even imagined, where I could sway my hips without the threat of physical violence. I wasn't a woman; I was just a boy who really, really, *really* liked playing Algernon. And who liked doing elaborate hair and makeup, donning a silk dressing gown or some other Victorian outfit, and swanning about, talking at length about feelings while holding a small elegant glass of sherry (or at least, something that we all agreed to pretend was sherry). But that didn't mean I was a woman. Right?

But I also was pretty clearly trans during adolescence, even on those occasions when I was not portraying Algernon in *The Importance of Being Earnest*. (And while I spent way more of my adolescence portraying Algernon in *The Importance of Being Earnest* than you can imagine, on any given day it was never more than a couple of hours.) My dysphoria, my alienation from my own body, was far more intense once my body started betraying me, going along with the boys, doing what they did, growing hair, and lowering my voice and so on. Did I know I was trans? I don't know, but I was certain enough that something was wrong that I never really dated anyone until I was twenty-five. There were a handful of fumbling attempts, including a homecoming dance with Nikki Jomantas at which I refused to dance, and a self-sabotaging love poem to a crush who was unavailable and wouldn't have responded to that kind of gesture anyway.

Every couple of years I'd force myself to ask someone out, go on a single date that would be roughly 75 percent awkward pauses, and then crawl back into my hole like Punxsutawney Phil seeing his shadow. The obstacle I couldn't surmount was that I couldn't imagine anyone wanting to date me.

My dysphoria wasn't the only reason for that, but it was the main one. I hated my body, hated the way it looked, the shape it had, the texture of its skin, everything. If I liked a girl, then how could I justify asking her to look at or, God forbid, touch this droopy awkward mess I inhab-

ited? Girls deserved better than me. They deserved someone who knew how to play by boy rules, someone who
could pass a test in the only subject I always failed (well,
that and penmanship). I was good at everything except
having a body.

And so that's where things were, forever. As far as I
was aware. My body could only ever be a source of shame
and weakness and embarrassment. I developed elaborate
rules for interacting with it, like a scientist working with a
deadly disease in the lab. As often as I needed to, I would
put on the hazmat suit and do some maintenance: get a
haircut, buy a new pair of black Converse Chuck Taylor
All Star high-tops, allow myself to be photographed at a
family gathering or work event, shave, fill in my height/
weight/sex/hair color/eye color on a form, create a social
media profile.

Even when I met Kelly, nothing changed. She was
raised in the same environment as I was and had many of
the same issues; our running joke was "When will we be
able to give up on this physical plane and become beings
of pure energy?"

Then, in 2011, I was in a production of Shakespeare's
A *Midsummer Night's Dream,* in the role of Francis

Flute, who pretends to be a woman for part of the play. This character's costume included a dress I needed to flitter and twitter and curtsy in, with a long-haired wig and extremely dramatic makeup. And one night, a stray thought crossed my mind.

What if I just wore a dress, like, all the time?

And then:

What if I wore it out at, like, a restaurant and did all the swishing and swaying I did as Algernon, and as Francis Flute, just because I wanted to?

Fireworks. Explosions. Cats and dogs jumping up and down. Crowds of people cheering.

Whoa. Okay. That was a surprisingly intense feeling, and I didn't know *what* to do about it. This would have been a fantastic time to realize I was trans, but nope, that still didn't seem like a possibility. Because trans people *know*, right? That's the story? They know from the moment they are born that they are in the wrong body?

Well, apparently not. At least, I didn't. It took me a while. But that feeling couldn't be ignored. Once the idea entered my head, it didn't want to leave. My struggle *not* to know was getting harder.

Some people refer to a person who is trans but doesn't

yet know it as an "egg," and, at the time, that applied to me. But the egg was cracked, and the crack was widening. There were feathers and a beak sticking out, and I wasn't going to be able to hold on to that shell much longer.

A few months later, the following thoughts struck me: I *never* wanted to wear the boy clothes again that I'd hated my entire life. I wanted to wear things that were pretty. And I knew if I made that change, people would need an explanation. And the only explanation that would make sense would be this truth: I am trans. I am a woman. I wear the clothes that were meant for me all along. I was going to have to come out of the closet.

So when did I know I was trans? Always. Never. But honestly? The *when* doesn't much matter. All I care about is that it isn't a secret. And it no longer is, so I am sharing it with you.

CHAPTER SIX

What Is Your Name?

"Why are names so important?"
"What is a deadname?"
"How did you choose the name Amy?"

Before I start the story of this chapter, I need to explain my deadname, which is a term some trans people use for the name they were given at birth. Since most (given) names are gender coded, people who do not identify as the gender they were assigned will often also not identify with the name they were given and choose a new one for themselves. Like most trans people, I find it a little uncomfortable to talk about. So if you know any trans people and are curious about what their name used to be, remember the word "deadname" and that it might not be something they want to talk about, unless they bring it up first. However, in my case, I've grown comfortable talking about my deadname (which is Tom, as you'll see later on in this chapter). It's part of my history, which I'm choosing to share with you. Now that I've explained that, I'll get back to my story, which starts at a birthday party. . . .

Birthdays made me nervous at the best of times, and this one had more riding on it than usual. It was the first time I had ever planned my own birthday party. It was a fear shared by likely anyone who has ever planned a party: *What if nobody shows up?* A decent number of people had said they would be there, but my mind reliably went straight to worst-case scenarios, and there were reasonable causes for concern. My birthday parties, since they were always on or near Memorial Day, usually struggled to attract guests, who often had other plans for the holiday weekend. Moreover, the one common bond among my guests was that they all lived in the Bay Area, home of free spirits, meaning that you can never assume that anybody won't flake on you until they actually walk through the door.

But there was yet another reason I was nervous in the hour or two before the party was to start, a reason that

I hadn't expected when I got up that morning: this was going to be the first time any of them would see me in my girl clothes. For a few months leading up to that birthday, I had been changing from boy to girl every time I was alone. As soon as I walked through the door after work, off would come the jeans and the T-shirt with "ironic" text written on it (my favorite was one from H&M that just said NOT ANOTHER STUPID TEXT T-SHIRT over and over all the way down the front), and on would come a skirt and a nice top.

When I woke up on weekends, I would lie in bed happily thinking about what outfit I would wear that day, mentally going through the clothes I'd accumulated from brief darts into the women's clothing section at Target, clothes that I kept hidden in a drawer, despite there being nobody in my apartment to hide them from. On the morning of my party, I decided on a black blouse with white polka dots and a denim skirt, along with some cute sandals. But I assumed that, prior to anyone's arrival, I'd take all those things off, hide them away, and put on some jeans and whichever T-shirt I pulled out of the laundry basket.

When the time came for my costume change . . . I

couldn't do it. It had been clear to me since February, at the latest, that I was trans, and that, as such, there was no alternative but to be open about it. If I didn't, if I kept it a secret in any way, then I would always have to keep some boy clothes around to wear in front of whoever I was still hiding myself from. Therefore, at some point, I was going to have to let my friends see me in my real clothes. But, not to put too fine a point on it, I was terrified.

Or rather, *more* terrified, since just a few months earlier, Kelly and I had gotten divorced, and every single one of my relationships had been put in jeopardy. How many of my friends were friends with "Tom," and how many of them were just friends with "Kelly's husband"? I still didn't feel I knew the answer. Kelly had always been in charge of our social life, which had been just fine with me. I'd always considered myself to be an introvert. Social situations gave me anxiety. But leaving Kelly in charge meant that all "our" friends were in some sense really "her" friends.

And now I was supposed to add yet another obstacle? I wasn't "Kelly's husband" anymore, but now was I not even "Tom"? Some new person—a woman whose name I didn't even know yet? How could I count on anyone to still care about me? How could I know that there would be anyone left to offer me support or understanding, or even just want me on their trivia team? It seemed too bold to add this new burden on everyone I knew, and it was hard to believe any of my relationships would survive this new demand I was making of them.

And yet.

The people (if any!) who would come to this party were the only people left in the world who I could count on for anything, the only people I could ever turn to if things went wrong. Even if they were only coming to this party out of obligation, I knew I could count on that same sense of pity if I ever needed someone to help me in an emergency. So I thought I needed to hide this from them in case they rejected me completely.

I was shocked to discover that, somehow, none of that mattered. This fear that had been ruling my life for as long as I could remember had suddenly met its match. Even if it meant that my friends were repulsed and confused, abandoning me and leaving me friendless and alone. Even that, in that moment, seemed like a better option than putting on a pair of baggy, shapeless jeans and some fake-vintage *Star Wars* T-shirt I'd bought at

Target. If that was the price I had to pay to feel any kind of human connection, it wasn't worth it. I'd been alone before, and I could do it again if I had to, but if so, I was going to be alone in a cute outfit!

It was a weird position to put my friends in. I'd never mentioned to any of them that I had any discomfort with my gender presentation. At least I'd tried hard not to give any indication, and at the time I thought I'd been successful. When they showed up and I was suddenly wearing a skirt with a cute top, I wasn't going to offer any explanation, because I still didn't have one.

I wasn't coming out that day; on some level I still didn't believe that I ever would. I assumed I would just keep living in denial of my own gender and sexuality, just as I'd been taught, and just as I believed everyone did. I had no expectations or even hopes for what my friends' reaction would be. It was outside the scope of my imagination. But I had no choice. Their reaction was up to them.

Most of the people who said they would come came, more than I'd even hoped. My first solo birthday party was an actual party, with a bunch of cool people from different parts of my life, some of whom I'd never thought would show. There were no awkward silences. I'd planned some activities for my guests, while still allowing people to fall into natural conversation groups and ignore the activity of the moment if they wanted.

As I realized the party was a success, it occurred to me that the only thing I was disappointed about was the very thing that I'd thought I was hoping for, which was that nobody had made any comment about my clothes. Nobody had even seemed to notice, really, although that seemed unlikely. I knew I had put my friends in an odd social situation. I hadn't made any comment on my clothes myself. I hadn't offered an explanation, or even acknowledged that I'd made a pretty dramatic change, stylistically speaking. I didn't have a clear explanation to give, and I was so afraid of rejection that I didn't want to raise the topic myself. But it was a huge moment in my life, and when they ignored it completely for better or worse, it left me feeling slightly disconnected from them, even as I was thrilled that the party was going smoothly.

The last guest to arrive was Jenn. She was my newest friend of the group. We'd only hung out a couple of times, and I might not have even invited her if I hadn't been trying to make sure I had enough people showing up. I went down to the lobby of my building to let her in, we greeted each other with a hug, and she stepped back and said, "I like your outfit!"

"Thanks," I said, blushing slightly. "The elevator's over here." We headed up and joined the party.

It's been more than six years since that day, and though Jenn is still late to everything, I believe she is the only person from that party with whom I'm still close. On my journey through transition, she gave me so many gifts, and so much support, and I will forever be grateful to her for all of it. But the first thing she did was maybe the most important: one acknowledgment, one compliment, one sign of acceptance was all I needed. From that moment, I knew I was doing the right thing. I knew I would be okay.

And of course, everyone's pathway is different. What I share, who I share it with, and when I share it are all personal to me, and nobody should have the right to influence those decisions. I think it's important not to even impose your acceptance on somebody and simply try to meet people where they are at any given time on their own path. I definitely saw that during one part of my transition in particular, my journey through changing my name.

I was christened Thomas Ezekiel Schneider. I was

Tommy as a kid. Then in first grade I was Thomas, because Mrs. Coleman called everybody by the name on their birth certificate. So she called Tony Niccolini "Antonio," that sort of thing. I assumed that in second grade I would get to be Tommy again, but when I showed up on the first day of class, there was a new kid there who had also been christened Thomas. His dad had been transferred to the local air force base, and our teacher said that, because it was hard to be the new kid, he would get to choose what name he wanted. He chose Tommy, and I was stuck with Tom. I lowkey resented him for that for years.

That first day of second grade was, as far as I was aware, the last chance I was ever going to have to pick my own name. I mean, not really—I knew plenty of kids who changed their name. Julie decided to be Julia. Samantha became Sam. Bill became Alex (it was his middle name). Even some of the grown-ups in my life had changed their name; I had two unrelated aunts who were known by different names to the outside world than they were within our family. But the only options I was aware of were Tom, Thomas, and Tommy. Tommy had been stolen from me. Thomas felt like somebody I'd never met. Tom it was.

And then, fast-forward a few decades, Tom it wasn't. It became clear to me that Tom was not my name. Or at least that the name Tom would lead people to assume that I was a boy. Now, that wasn't the only thing that had led people, myself included, to assume that I was a boy for my entire life. But any of the other things that might be changed when I was older (when or if they could be changed at all) would involve a significant investment of time, energy, money, makeup, medicines, or extensive surgical intervention.

Changing my name, however, at least in casual conversation among close friends, was something I could do fairly easily. And while I knew Tom did not feel like the right name for me . . . what was?

I struggled with it for a long time. It felt unending. It's a strange feeling, going through life without a name. One of the first times I'd gone out in semipublic dressed as a woman was to a backyard concert at the house of Nora and Ann, this slightly older lesbian couple I knew. At some point during the party, Nora took an opportunity to ask me privately, "I just wanted to check, am I still calling you Tom? Are you still using he/him pronouns?"

"I have no idea," I said. "I don't know what you should

call me or what I'm doing or anything. I just . . . I just wanted to wear this outfit. I don't know what's going on with me at all."

And that was it for the time being. She was understanding and didn't demand further explanation. That wasn't true of everyone. One time, my friend Jessie and I were hanging out at a friend's house, chatting about my identity, and he decided that I needed to be pushed. In a very well-intentioned way, he started getting in my face: "You know what? You need to stop debating this—you know what your name is. You know! You know what it is! Stop being all, like, 'Um, well, uh, I don't know.' Just decide! Listen, I'm going to ask you right now: What's your name? Now, what name popped into your head? Whatever it is, that's the right one. Come on, you've got to do this now!" It was a bizarre moment, having somebody attempt to bully me into doing something empowering. In any case, it wasn't the right time.

I actually *did* have a name pop into my head, not that I was going to tell him that. It was a name I'd liked ever since I was a kid, the one I'd used in my head the first time my egg cracked, the first time I imagined introducing myself as a woman. *Jenny.* And I know some trans people who would say, "Well, that's it; that's the name you gave yourself in childhood; that's your real name and always has been." But somehow, it didn't feel right. I mean, part of it was that I had a friend named Jenn, and I didn't want two leading characters in the story of my life to have such similar names. That seemed confusing. And apart from that: sure, I'd liked the name Jenny when I was a kid, but that was because it was a kid's name. I wasn't a little girl. I never had been, and I never would be. I needed a name for my grown-up self.

Apart from the gender coding, I'd liked the name Tom just fine, after I got over my resentment of that seven-year-old name thief. (Just kidding, I'm still not over it.) Tom was short and generic, easy to spell, and easy to pronounce. People didn't associate anything in particular with it, as far as I knew. It felt like with the name Tom you could be any age, do anything for a living. That was what I was looking for in a name. I went through a few rounds of trying out candidates, having Jenn or my therapist try calling me Michelle or Alice or whatever, but none of them felt right.

I don't even remember where or when I came up with Amy, but that's part of why I know it was the right choice. It came into my brain, and it just fit. It wasn't inspired by anything in particular; it didn't mean anything in particular, any more than Tom ever had. It was just a name, not hard to write, not hard to spell out loud. Alternative spellings existed, but the A-M-Y version was dominant enough not to require specifying, any more than I'd needed to specify that my name was Tom rather than Thom before. It meant what I wanted it to mean: nothing.

That's something I think people can misunderstand about trans people, trans women in particular. For much of my life, "drag queen" and "trans woman" were understood to mean the same thing, and so, like everyone else, I assumed that trans-ness was about exoticizing femininity, about wanting to be big and bold and femme and have dramatic hair and makeup and be brash and enticing and intoxicating. That hasn't been completely absent from my experience, especially when I was starting out. When I first came out, it was as if I'd been a kid standing with my face pressed to the window of a candy store for thirty years, and once I was allowed in, I wanted *everything*.

But when that rush settled down, I realized that wasn't what it was about at all. Sure, I liked glitter, sparkles, high heels, bold lips, dramatic eye shadow. But that was just accessorizing. One item of clothing that called to me early on was a shirt I saw at Target: a shapeless workout/errands/sleep top that said MESSY BUN/TARGET RUN/GET IT DONE. That was what I wanted, to live my whole life simply as myself, including the vast majority of it when I wasn't doing anything interesting or girly or exciting. I just wanted to be, well, Amy. That was all.

The final stage of my coming out, the moment that I use to mark my "traniversary," was coming out at work. The reason this was the final stage was not that my coworkers were the people I was most frightened to come out to; I was fortunate enough to be working with a great bunch of people, and though there were one or two engineers who I thought might be a little weird about it (they weren't—they were great!), I didn't foresee any major problems.

Well, I mean, I did, in a sense. I foresaw all sorts of disastrous outcomes about everything at this time in my life. I just mean that, when my brain presented me with various catastrophic scenarios that might ensue from coming out to my coworkers, I didn't really think they could happen. But it still felt weird. It still felt like I was talking about something I shouldn't be talking about at work. Nonetheless, I needed to do it; I needed to stop having to haul out this ugly, ill-fitting boy costume every day just to do my job.

We had our weekly staff meeting on Friday afternoons, and that meeting was clearly the right occasion for this announcement. For a few weeks I kept deciding that next Friday would be the one and then finding a reason to wait another week. But then one Friday, instead of having our meeting, we had one of our quarterly "offsites," the equivalent of when your class gets to have a pizza party because they raised the most money during a fundraiser.

I was having a good time with my work friends and feeling brave. I came out to one of my closest friends there and told her I planned to come out to everyone else the following Friday, but I asked her to keep it to herself until then. So now I had to do it; otherwise, she would start feeling uncomfortable about keeping the secret, and I couldn't do that to my girl Candace!

So the day came: June 30, 2017. There was a portion of the meeting where everyone was invited to bring up any points for discussion that they wanted, and I raised my hand. I'd rehearsed this moment over and over again for the last few weeks, getting it down word for word. I knew everyone in that meeting; I trusted them all; I didn't see how it could go wrong. Yet I was terrified. I think it was just that this was it. This was the last chance for it all to come crashing down, for some negative consequence of my transition to turn out to be so bad that I had to just scrap the whole thing and crawl back into my shell. I mean, the shell was broken into a million pieces and scattered all around the coop by then, but I still thought it could happen.

I was trembling as I stood up, and my voice shook, but I forced out the lines I'd been rehearsing. It sounded like "Hey, so, when all of you met me, I introduced myself to you as a man named Tom. But for the last few months, outside of this office, I've been introducing myself to everyone as a woman named Amy. And that's how I see myself now. I've been hiding this at work. Well, not completely hiding it."

I held up my hand, which was shaking, to show off my manicure. I'd been painting my nails for a few months by that point; when asked about it, I would say something like "Oh, you know, I just felt like I wanted to do some weird San Francisco thing. It's fun!" So this was my acknowledgment to my coworkers that my explanation had never made any sense, and we'd all kind of known it. I said a few more sentences, partly just around some practical details involving my email address, and something about how, as a software engineer, I know that two different pointers can refer to the same value, and so if people called me Tom, I would know what they meant. It was a solid work coming-out speech. Self-deprecating, professional, to the point, didn't waste too much meeting time. Being so nervous wasn't ideal, but that's why I'd made sure to write myself some good lines, to paper over the weak performance.

And . . . that was that. It was done. Everybody said the right things and meant them. The meeting ended, and I went back to one of our single-person bathrooms, where, for the last time, I took off my stupid pants and my baggy, ugly T-shirt and my boxer briefs—basically that whole costume that never felt right and I'd been lugging around forever. Then I put on the clothes, my *real* clothes, I'd brought in my backpack; put on some makeup (I wasn't great at it, but I did my best); and finished out the workweek.

The last chance for disaster had come. Disaster hadn't happened. I was free.

On the one-year anniversary of their hire date, every employee was given a coffee mug with the company logo and their name on it. I'd gotten mine a few months earlier, which bummed me out, but whatever, it was just a coffee mug. A few days after I came out, though, our office manager walked up to my desk, carrying a box. "Hey, Amy, this just came for you." She pulled out a coffee mug. Just like the one I had. Company logo on one side. And on the other side: my name. Amy. If it was on my coffee mug at work, it had to be real. It's an amazing feeling to get (or give) a gift that makes someone feel really understood!

CHAPTER SEVEN

How Can I Be Fully Myself?

"Have you ever been bullied?"
"How do you cope with ADD?"
"Why do you talk about theater so much?"

Learning how to be true to yourself can be hard. It means not buying into other people's perceptions of who you are. It may also mean figuring out things about yourself you might not yet understand. Most of my life I never considered that I might have ADD, or attention deficit disorder. (The technical talk for this, according to the Centers for Disease Control and Prevention, is a person who may have trouble paying attention or controlling impulsive behaviors, act without thinking about what the result will be, or be overly active.)

I thought of ADD as meaning "ill-behaved," and I

certainly wasn't ill-behaved. I behaved great. I crushed it at being well-mannered. Having ADD was a lot like being trans. I never thought it could be true of me, because I was a good kid, and kids with ADD—and trans kids— were bad kids. (Having ADD wasn't quite as bad as being trans, to be sure.) And my mom was vocal in her belief in the nonexistence of ADD. Some kids were just naughty was how she looked at it. Though to her credit, she never judged them for it. It wasn't the kids' *fault* that they were naughty, and she understood why people had felt the need to invent a term for it that sounded less judgmental. She just wasn't going to pretend it was something differ- ent. As a teacher, she saw accommodations for ADD as just another excuse, an attempt to get an advantage over the other students.

Most people agreed with her back then. But by the time my brother got diagnosed with ADD in college, my mom was ready to accept it. She had seen throughout his academic career that his grades didn't match his under- standing of the material. He had to consider everything from every angle. When he would take a test, he would get a reasonably high percentage of correct answers on the first third of the test, which is as far as he would get before time was up. Giving him longer to finish the test wasn't about giving him an advantage over the other students; it was giving the teacher the opportunity to better assess what he had learned. My mom's reaction surprised me, although I had long felt that ADD was a perfectly legitimate diagnosis. I mean, for other people, not for me. I knew my issue: I was just plain lazy.

As I saw it, my story went this way: I happened to be born with a brain suited for school. All through grade school, I had the best grades in the class, and I didn't even have to work for them. Then when I got to high school, the work grew a little more difficult. I realized that I could either start working hard and continue having the very best grades, or continue being lazy and just have very good grades. And being lazy seemed like the way to go, so that's what I did. But that wasn't a convincing story. Much like my "I'm not trans; I'm just a boy who wishes with every fiber of his being that he was a girl" is not a convincing story. I remember sitting in my living room my freshman year of high school, looking at my geometry homework and crying. I was crying not because the homework was hard, but because it was easy. Math came to me particularly easily (until I took differential equations in college, at which point math just completely stopped making any sense). There was no reason why I couldn't just do this assignment. And yet, I wasn't doing it, and I couldn't understand why. Laziness was the only reason I could come up with. I placed the blame on the same place as always: me.

Having undiagnosed ADD sucks, y'all. What I've learned about it is that if you have ADD, your brain doesn't process dopamine (a chemical messenger naturally released from nerve cells in your brain) very well. The kind of default background levels of dopamine we naturally get just don't do the trick. You know how you feel when you're really, really bored? That's my default. In Dungeons and Dragons terms, I always take +2 damage from boredom relative to an unmodified character. That's why ADD is treated with medication that provides your brain enough dopamine so it can feel the same way a non-ADD brain feels all the time. It makes me feel calm. It stops the raging of my brain's constant demands for more stimulation.

While it doesn't make me feel wired up, it does make me feel like I have a superpower. The first time I tried medication, I was in my messy apartment and noticed some underwear lying on the floor. I thought, *I should put that in the hamper.* And, get this, *I actually did it.* I just picked it up, carried it over to the hamper, and put it in, simply because I'd decided to. I was blown away. That was an entirely new experience for me. Was this how other people lived their lives? They could just decide to do something and then do it, without having to argue with themselves for a while? I saw the answer to a mystery that had always baffled me: How did people keep their homes clean? I'd never been able to imagine what that would be like.

Having ADD can also mean that you never fully develop object permanence. When you can't see something, you'll lose all knowledge of what it is or where it is. Having piles on a shelf might look messier than having everything tucked away in a drawer, but if something is tucked in a drawer, I might as well not own it. I also tend to abandon projects. I've got a bunch of painting materials somewhere, a partially finished adult coloring book somewhere else, perhaps under my half-completed latch-hook wall hanging. I just came across my guitar and thought, *Boy, I haven't picked this up in forever.* Then I spent half an hour trying to tune it, replaced one of the strings, and then put it down and haven't picked it up since. I've written the first third of multiple screenplays. I made a stop-motion animation film once that's five seconds long. I get into something, buy all the supplies, do it for a bit, and then hit a wall with it and don't care about it at all.

It interacts with my depression, too. When it comes to mental health, or literally anything else, everything is connected. My ADD gave my depression so many great talking points when it wanted to recite a list of my failings to me while I was trying to sleep. Depression in turn takes away your interest in the world around you, which means you don't have the dopamine your brain needs. Medication can help mitigate the worst of it, but it doesn't *fix* it.

Then again, how much of it is something that needs to be fixed? I mean, there's no way I would have been so good at *Jeopardy!* without ADD. ADD made me literally addicted to learning. My brain needs stimulation, and that's one of the best non-self-destructive ways to get it. I'm not great at learning a lot about any one thing, because that gets boring, and I end up tossing it on the pile with my juggling equipment and half-finished paintings. But *Jeopardy!* doesn't reward that level of detail anyway; it values variety.

I value it too! I *like* all my abandoned projects. They each gave me what I wanted out of them. I wrote six songs in college and haven't written one since, but I'm still proud of them. I know that other languages can indicate number in more ways than just singular and plural. (Finnish has a separate form just for things that are in pairs, like legs or sides of a coin.) If someone were to say to me, "Okay, we've got this new treatment that completely eliminates whatever this ADD thing is," I wouldn't take it. I like having the medication that fixes the most inconvenient part of it, but I don't want it to change. I'd still rather have it untreated than have it taken away. That is one way I have learned to truly accept myself for who I am.

Another thing I have learned is to try to keep my circumstances from defining who I am. Many of us grow up in environments we wish we could change, or with people—no matter how much we love them—we wish we could change. Maybe some of those people have even hurt us—whether intentionally or unintentionally—or we feel we have to change who *we* are to accommodate them. It's hard to see another way out of that thinking sometimes, especially when we are kids, but it is possible.

I've already shared that my mom was a great teacher, and there were a lot of other wonderful things about her too. But not everything was great, and I grew up in a house where I was coping with a mother dealing with alcoholism. I was nine when I was first made aware of her illness and she was admitted to the hospital, and I didn't believe my dad at first. Like, she was obviously the greatest mom in the entire world: the most beautiful, the kindest, the smartest, the most fun. I was so lucky to have her! Yet nobody else in the family seemed to really share my opinion. Over time, I could see for myself how much she was struggling, and I had mixed emotions about how she was handling it.

My mother has been sober ever since, but for decades I denied that any of the failings I saw in her could have affected my life in any way. Then I started realizing how many of her "headaches" corresponded with family gatherings she didn't want to attend, that she was just bailing on them. I would remember my dad making excuses: "Betty's not feeling well." I hated to see how embarrassed he was when he said it, and I hated even more how embarrassed it made me when I was forced to go along with a story that I didn't believe, to look like a goof who didn't know my mom was faking it. From age ten to eighteen, I remember many times when we were heading out to something, or even just about to sit down to dinner, and she'd say, "Oh, I'm not feeling well. My head hurts. I'm going to go lie down."

I would think, *Well, maybe it's true—maybe you're not feeling well, but guess what? You haven't been feeling well in years. You need to figure out how to live with it and show up. Be part of the family.*

When I was married to Kelly, on multiple occasions one of my relatives, usually one who had married into the family, took Kelly aside and said, "Here's what you need to know about Betty." They told Kelly stories from my childhood that I'd never heard, stories about her drinking, stories that made her sound like, well . . . an alcoholic.

That felt like a betrayal to me. Why did nobody ever really tell *me* about Betty? I wanted to yell at them: *You all saw me being raised in chaos. Why didn't anybody ever talk to me about it? Why didn't anybody ever help me understand my conflicted feelings about my mother?* That hurt.

A year or two after meeting Kelly, I was cast in a play by a friend of hers. Through the theater department she was attending, students could put on their own plays, and one of them invited me to play a role in their production. As a community theater veteran, to be considered worthy of acting alongside these people who took theater so much more seriously than I did was a huge ego boost. I think I'm being honest when I say I did a great job! I absolutely felt like I belonged on that stage. It remains one of my fondest theater memories.

But the other memory I have is after the play, when the house lights went up and I looked out into the audience and saw my dad and brother there. But not her. My dad told me my mom's stomach wasn't feeling well, with that same embarrassed grin I'd seen a thousand times before, and my heart sank. I was so upset at myself. But I couldn't reason myself out of the pain I was feeling. What did this whole experience teach me? I'm not sure.

I'm still figuring that out. But I've come a long way. And the main reason I've come so far is that, a few weeks after that night when I stood with my father and brother, fighting back tears, I walked into the office of a stranger and said, "Well, I'm not really sure about this. I don't think I really need therapy. But a few weeks ago, something happened with my mom. . . ."

I've made a lot of good decisions in my life. That one might have been the best. If you've ever considered seeking therapy, please do it. It might take you a few tries, but it can transform your life in ways you aren't even imagining and really help you learn to be true to yourself.

And now we're back to talking about theater, because, let's face it, there are a whole lot of life lessons that come from doing theater! I liked theater from the first play I ever did (*The Music Man*), but I didn't fall in love with theater until a couple of years later, at a summer camp in southern Ohio. It was their annual performing arts camp, a ten-day experience where we would show up, audition for and get cast in a musical, spend a week rehearsing it, and then perform it for our parents when they came to pick us up. I knew about it because my older cousins had attended it in years past. When they'd been there, the musicals put on were legit, recognizable shows like *Pippin* or *The Fantasticks*, shows that people had at some point willingly paid money to see (probably not to see performed by children, but still). By the time I was old enough to attend, however, they had switched over to shows that they didn't have to spend money on to use (you have to pay to perform certain plays), which limited the choices. That summer, they had selected *K.I.D.S. Radio*, the plot of which consists of a bunch of children disputing how to run their school's radio station (I know, I know—a tale as old as time!).

Okay, so it was silly, but I didn't really care, and we all had a ton of fun with it. My character was a fussy Italian opera star, and while I only had one scene, it included a whole solo song, which only a few of us got to do. It was before my voice changed, and I was still a halfway decent singer, and an all-the-way confident one. The song was set to the tune of "Largo al factotum," from *The Barber of Seville* (which sounds super random, but if you ask Siri to play it, there's a good chance you've heard it before), but with lyrics about a misbehaving dog (you're laughing already, right?).

I still remember some of the lyrics: "I have a dog and his name is-a Figaro. / He barks at the milkman, the mailman he barks—Ah, so!" I could go on, but I will spare us both.

At this point I was twelve or thirteen years old, an

age at which children have learned how to be hurtful to each other. You might think I'd have been embarrassed to do something so ridiculous in public. But I had already learned some lessons about how to deflect bullies, and one of them was this: Never play their game. Play your own.

Whenever somebody tried to make fun of me, I would just shrug, as if I was disappointed in them for not understanding what was really going on. What I have learned, slowly, is this vital truth. Even if we're right, even if people around us are sometimes thoughtless, judging and attacking us for reasons that they themselves cannot comprehend, incapable of seeing the pain they cause us—even then, they are still just . . . people. Just like us. Even when they hurt us, the answer is not to shut them all out, because they are hurting too, and the only way to deal with our pain is to try to help them deal with theirs. I don't want to imply that this was completely successful. I certainly still got bullied. But I had some success, and it kept me from the absolute bottom of the social pecking order. The key is this: you can't look like you think there's anything wrong. You can't buy into their framing, to admit that there's anything there for you to be embarrassed about. Never admit to being embarrassed about anything, even (especially) when you are. And that's my advice for how to survive middle school: keep everyone off balance and confused long enough for you to escape.

When I performed that song, I knew the only way to approach it was to go all in: big voice, big hand gestures, big emotions. It was a hit; the counselors were loving it in rehearsal, and none of the other kids teased me about it at all. We had our performance for the parents at the end of the week, and not to brag (definitely bragging), but I stole the show. I got the biggest reaction, the most applause, the least forced laughter. It's hard to capture how thrilling it is to know that you've won over a live audience, particularly a skeptical one. It was my first experience of it, and it was a thrill that I'd never forget. In fact, five-ish years later, in high school English class, we had an assignment: write about a moment from your life that stands out as an extremely vivid memory, and I wrote about that performance. Hey, I'm writing about it now!

There were other things that made it such a peak experience in my life. It was a beautiful summer day, at the end of a week I'd enjoyed intensely, out in nature, with kids my own age, with songs, and four square, and conversations about our feelings. But the main thing about that performance was that I had been good at it, hands down. Before that day, the only thing I'd been really certain I was good at was school—homework and tests and spelling bees and such. I was proud of all that, to an extent. But it felt too easy. I didn't feel like I deserved that much credit for academic success. This performance was different. I'd gotten some validation from previous performances, but I'd just been doing what I was told. This time, I knew that the audience was approving of something I had created. I'd made daring character choices, committed to them, and then stood alone onstage and blown the audience away. For once in my life, I was actually proud.

Onstage, you can get away with anything. You can do the very things that frighten you the most, and not only can you survive them, but you can enjoy them. You can feel proud, even about the things you're most ashamed of. It's no coincidence that the LGBTQ+ community is wildly overrepresented among theater kids. Being queer so often means being ashamed of your queerness. It means feeling driven to express a part of yourself, even though you know that it's prohibited, a part you're ashamed even to have. Theater gives you a chance to express that prohibited self, right out in the open, but in a deniable way—that wasn't me violating my prescribed gender norms! I was just playing a character! *wink*

Theater often provides exposure to literature and opinions and people that are vastly different from the ones you are used to—especially if you grow up in a socially conservative environment. Remember my "this is *theater*" experience? I might not have had the benefit of that moment if I hadn't done drama—or it might have taken many more years for me to have that kind of experience.

Not only is acting a refuge from judgment, it can also be a refuge from yourself. I have not been a big fan of myself for most of my life. I kept a mental list of all my shortcomings, all my failures, everything I had to feel ashamed of, and I tended that list with great care, always on the lookout for opportunities to add to it. It was a relief not to be me for a while every night, not to have any responsibility for myself or my actions. Left to my own devices, it seemed like I always did the wrong thing or said the wrong thing, and I always would, because I was internally flawed somehow. But in a play, some things aren't up to you. The script tells you what to say, the director tells you what to do, and for a brief period you don't have to drag yourself for always making the wrong decision, because you're not making any decisions at all.

That's a lot of what theater meant to me. When you think of actors, you probably don't think of shy, timid, introvert types like I was back then. You probably picture big, brash personalities, always putting themselves at the center of attention. And for good reason, because those people are also drawn to the stage, and with motives that are almost the opposite of the ones I've just described. The way I put it is that, generally, two types of people are attracted to theater: people who always want to be seen and people who always want to be hidden. In theater, you can do both at once.

Theater is a place where you can stand alone on a stage, with hundreds of people focusing their full attention on you, and yet still be invisible. It's a place where you can say, "Hey! Everybody! Drop what you're doing and look at me! Notice what I'm doing! Stop thinking about your own life and focus on what I am feeling right now!" and yet somehow say it selflessly, humbly, as part of a communal project. Theater brings together people who, offstage, might find each other intolerable, and offers them each what they need. For the shy, it offers escape, concealment, and safety. For the confident, it offers attention, freedom, validation. In theater, not only can you do the very things you fear the most, but you can do them with the very people who make you fear those things. Weirdly, it's the place where you can pretend to be someone else while fully showing the world your true self.

Putting on a play is like a massive group trust fall, with everyone involved in the production constantly falling, even as they constantly catch one another. If you do the thing you're afraid of, and do it together with the people who make you afraid of it, then eventually you'll start to realize that you no longer have anything to fear.

As the saying goes, "The show must go on!" This has to do with so much more than theater. It has to do with how you show up for yourself throughout your life. We all have so many opportunities to make choices for ourselves, little and big, every single day. Perhaps our most important lesson is to learn how to make those choices in service to being true to ourselves as often as we possibly can. What choices will you make that will help you fully be the person you are—and the person you want to become?

CHAPTER EIGHT

What's It Like to Be Famous?

"How does it feel to be so successful?"
"What are you going to do with the money?"
"What does it mean to be a trans spokesperson?"

can't speak for you, but if I were reading this book, this is the part I'd be most interested in: the part about being famous. My whole life I had wondered: What would it be like to be one of those people? The winners. The people who hit the jackpot, who go from normal life to that other kind, where your name is in headlines and your face is on TV, where you get recognized on the street, have your own fan club and Wikipedia page. How would that feel? No, but really, how would it actually feel?

I want to warn you right away: I still don't have an

answer to that question. I've gotten a lot closer, but this is all still so new. It has only been a couple of years since I found myself living my fantasy, years that passed like a whirlwind, a whirlwind that picked me up and carried me along with it, twisting and tumbling.

And I've loved it! I'd always wanted it, on some level. After all, that's the whole reason I wanted to know what it felt like! But I hadn't admitted that to myself. Officially, my feeling was that fame wasn't for me, that I'd be overwhelmed by it. When I married Kelly, who studied theater and publicly declared her intent to pursue some form of stardom, I thought I'd found the perfect solution. Kelly would be the star, and I would bask in the warmth of her stardom, without having to risk exposing myself to the glare of the public. My public image would consist of blushing modestly while Kelly thanked me in acceptance speeches for various awards, and that would be enough for me.

Well, that would have been enough for Tom. But I'm not Tom, and never was—that was just a character I played for thirty years or so. As the years go by, I've slowly started to unlearn some of the reflexive habits you develop when you immerse yourself in a role that way, so committed that you mistake acting choices for character traits. Particularly when those choices (modestly stating a distaste for fame, for example) have always been warmly received by those around you.

My belief in my own modesty had been getting shakier for years. Looking at myself in the mirror felt so good that it became harder and harder to believe that other people didn't get some enjoyment out of looking at me. The things I'd spent my whole life trying to avoid had all happened to me at once, and I'd survived! I'd done great! I couldn't be that bad, right? I still wasn't letting myself imagine that I could be famous and successful. But I had started to ponder the hypothesis that plenty of famous people must not have foreseen becoming famous until, one day, they were. And then, as 2021 turned into 2022, I went ahead and proved that hypothesis by becoming famous myself.

The instant that it happened, I realized I was ready, that I had been ready, that this was something I'd wanted all along. I first confronted the fact of my impending celebrity before anyone else knew it was coming, including my new girlfriend, Genevieve. I was down in LA, having won three games of *Jeopardy!* the week before, and having six days and two plane trips to think about it since then. I had done better than I thought I would, but I still wouldn't let myself believe that I could be that good.

Then I went to the studio that next Monday, and I won all five games I played—kind of convincingly. I didn't want to seem arrogant, to myself or anyone else. But the results spoke for themselves. I was already ranking high on the all-time lists. If I did the same thing the next day, which was possible, I would be quite high indeed, among the legends, just like that. That would mean that there would be people who would recognize my name and face for years to come, in the same way I recognized Julia Collins, James Holzhauer, Arthur Chu. I hadn't allowed myself to believe that could happen when I arrived at the studio that day and turned my phone off for the next ten or eleven hours. The only people who knew what had happened that day were the ones who were in the studio, and they had all signed nondisclosure agreements (NDAs), promising not to share any results until after the show aired on TV. After that last win, I had an hour or so to accept it for myself, apart from what anyone else would think. That's when I realized: I was ready. The last five years of my life had prepared me for fame.

Was I incredibly lucky? Sure. But I'd been incredibly lucky before. Luck was more prevalent in the universe than I had been led to believe. Being the beneficiary of good luck doesn't necessarily mean you don't deserve it. And I deserved it. I deserved it! That was a strange feeling, believing that I deserved something, but I liked it.

So yeah, that was the first answer I learned. How does fame feel? It feels great! A few months later, in February, I was flown out to DC, my first experience of celebrity treatment. Genevieve and I were slack-jawed the whole weekend at how amazing everything was. They flew us first class! With those sleep pods you can lie down in! They put us up in a swanky hotel, in a suite the size of our apartment, with floor-to-ceiling windows in the bedroom, and drapes that you could control with a switch from your bed! Genevieve's aunt, who lived in DC, texted her something along the lines of *Oh, well, that neighborhood isn't the real DC*, and we just laughed. Of course it wasn't! It wasn't the real anything. It was Rich People Town, a place we never thought we'd be invited to!

But it went beyond travel and accommodations. Fame comes with a lot of prizes. Companies just give you stuff, right when you can finally afford to pay for it.

They give it to you precisely because you can pay for it. It feels unfair on some level (and it definitely is), but listen: Genevieve and I both came from backgrounds where, while I wouldn't call us poor (we were never in much danger of being actually out on the street), we both knew how it felt to count the pennies in our bank account, and if people wanted to send us stuff, then by God we wanted to get it. We hired our friend Hilary to manage my Instagram, with the goal of getting us free stuff, and she delivered. Clothes, makeup, bath bombs, face masks. A trip to Ottawa. A toaster with a touch-screen interface, where you could select the item you were toasting and then choose from various pictures of that item to specify what level of toasted-ness you wanted to achieve, and it played a little song when it was done. Where did the toaster come from? Why was it sent to us? We had no idea, but we immediately started making more toast than we'd ever imagined.

The only social media I'd used heavily had been Twitter/X; years of effort had gotten me up to three hundred or four hundred followers, which was, you know, fine, but less than I felt like I deserved. But as the air-date of my first episode approached, I knew there would be some amount of scrutiny on me, so I locked down my account and made a new, public account, with the handle @Jeopardamy. (Still pretty proud of that, even if people consistently think it's @Jeopardyamy. It's a portmanteau—a word that blends the sounds and combines the meanings of two other words into one—like "brunch" [breakfast and lunch]!)

The day my first episode aired, Genevieve and I had gotten an Airbnb to host a watch party. After work, I headed over to the Airbnb to help set up. I was on the road at four p.m., which was when the episode started airing on much of the East Coast. My Twitter notifications started coming in. At first they were the trickle I'd been expecting. But around four fifteen, I was delayed getting to the Airbnb because, all of a sudden, I was getting Twitter notifications every second or two, in such a flood that I had no idea what Google Maps was expecting me to do. I took the next exit, pulled over to the side of the road, and turned off Twitter notifications. My first episode hadn't finished airing, and I already had more followers than I'd ever had before.

When my run of *Jeopardy!* episodes was in its second week, I was at the Safeway up on Pleasant Valley, buying our groceries for the week. While I was checking out, two different people recognized me and told me how much they were enjoying watching my run. They were maybe the fourth and fifth people to recognize me in public, something like that. I walked out the door of that Safeway grinning. I'd loved what had happened, both for the ego boost and for how nice it felt to have brightened people's days by doing nothing more than buying groceries. This was all amazing!

But then I had a realization: if it ever stopped being amazing, if there ever came a time when I would prefer to buy my groceries without strangers coming up to me, wanting to talk, and potentially noticing the unreasonably high percentage of potato-based products in my cart—if that time ever came, there was no way to turn it off. This was my life now, and for some amount of time to come. There's no pause button on fame simply because you want one.

The week my *Jeopardy!* run ended, I did a ton of interviews. I didn't have to; the *Jeopardy!* people made it clear that I was free to refuse any or all media requests. But I'd discovered my inner diva, and I wanted to put as much Amy out there as the market would bear. I found myself saying things like "Ugh, I'm going to have to get up so early for this *Good Morning America* interview." #relatable

As the week went on, I answered the same three questions (see the beginning of this chapter) in a seemingly endless parade of five-minute interviews. I had the experience that's familiar to celebrities, as well as anybody who's worked in the service industry: saying the same phrases so often that at times I couldn't even tell whether I was saying anything at all or just spouting a bunch of gibberish. Whether the phrase is "Thank you for your patience!" or "You know, I'd watched the show my whole life, and I thought I could be good, maybe win three or four games, but I could never have predicted anything like this!," it nonetheless loses all meaning.

I was speaking at an event in a hotel; I genuinely don't remember which event or which hotel, but I know I wasn't the main attraction. I was trying to take the elevator down to the street. An elevator arrived, but it was already packed. One of the people in front of me, the one who had pressed the down button, waved the people in that elevator away. "We'll get the next one." I nodded in agreement. The doors closed.

And then they reopened.

A voice from the back, I couldn't see who: "Are you Amy Schneider? From *Jeopardy!*?"

"Yeah, that's me!" My automated humble-gratified-pleasant response.

"I just want to say, my father passed away this year, cancer, and when he was in the hospital, we watched your whole run, and we all rooted you on together, he was such a huge fan, I mean, obviously it was such a hard time, but seeing you was so great, and then . . ."

I realized I needed to turn one of her commas into a period.

"I just wanted to acknowledge that, and—"

"Thank you so much; I really appreciate hearing that. Have a good day!"

The doors closed.

I was invited to the White House. Not to see the president, or the vice president. Trans rights haven't come that far yet. I'd meet with the Second Gentleman (the vice president's husband) and give some brief remarks in the Briefing Room, at the same podium where Allison Janney (excuse me, I mean fellow Daytonian Allison Janney) had stood in her role as C. J. Cregg, White House press secretary, in all those episodes of *The West Wing* I'd loved. The whole day was the same mixture of surreal and boring I'd always experienced in major life events. It didn't seem real, and yet it quite clearly was.

Nobody seemed to know what was going on. All the rooms were too old to have particularly effective climate control. Doors stuck. People scrambled to handle things they had previously believed somebody else was handling. The hairstyle I'd just had professionally done was torn to bits by unusually strong winds. I was a little gassy from breakfast for some reason. And yet it was also, you know, the White House. It looked just like it did on TV! And so, when I was standing at the podium and some reporters began asking me questions, I rolled with it (despite having been told a dozen times that they wouldn't ask me any questions).

C. J. Cregg could handle this. And so can I.

I conducted that briefing with aplomb.

At another podium in another town, I was standing on a stage in Portland, taking questions from the audience. One woman, having been called upon, began walking up to the stage. This wasn't part of the plan. I looked over at the moderator, who was looking at me with the same expression on her face as I suspected I had on mine. But it didn't look like this woman was about to hurt me or anything, so I guessed we were just going to roll with it.

"Hi, Amy, I don't really have a question; I just wanted to give you these."

She held out her hands, and I knelt down at the front of the stage to take what she was giving me. At first I thought it was just some rocks, until she put them in my hands, at which point I realized that it was in fact just some rocks. They had designs painted on them, which I couldn't process in the moment. The woman explained that they were fairy rocks, which, sure, that sounded like a thing. I smiled and thanked her, of course, and to be clear, it really is the thought that counts, and I'm grateful to this person, who only wanted to give me something in return for the joy that I had given her. But all I could think was *I am not flying home with a bunch of rocks in my luggage*. And I didn't. I hope those fairy rocks found their forever home eventually.

When, during the course of my time on *Jeopardy!*, I was mugged—it didn't have anything to do with being famous—I realized I wasn't going to be able to write some social media content I had publicly committed to.

I got on my laptop and posted something along the lines of *Just got robbed. I'm unharmed, they just took my purse and phone, but that means I won't be able to post much for a day or two.*

Within the next few hours, I got a bunch of concerned messages from friends and family. "Are you okay? I saw the headline." The headline? When I googled my name, there they were, a bunch of blaring headlines for articles that consisted of, essentially, the tweet I had just posted. I realized that if I didn't want something I did to be turned into a news article, I'd have to keep it private. My previously massive follower count started to feel intimidating rather than gratifying.

So how does fame feel? Complicated. That first thing I learned—that fame feels great—is still the first answer I reach for. When people recognize me and ask me for a selfie or something, occasionally they'll say something like "I'm sorry, you must get tired of all this." To which my response, always and sincerely, is "Strangers coming up and giving me compliments? How could I be tired of that?"

Of course, I'd considered this possibility in advance and thought of a variety of ways I could turn out to be tired of it. And many people do. Several other *Jeopardy!* champions have been quite clear that they don't enjoy it at all, and I do understand why. Whenever I'm out in public, I know that, at any moment, a stranger may come up and want to compliment me. Which again, to me, is usually a great feeling to have. But nonetheless, it is not always the feeling I'm in the mood for. When you're walking to the corner store to buy something to cheer you up after a falling out with a close friend, you might not necessarily want to take a selfie with a stranger. But you can't show it. I can't afford anyone telling negative stories about me. And I mean the word "afford" literally.

Because another lesson of fame is this: If you get famous enough to quit your job, that doesn't mean you've stopped working. It means that you are now a small-business owner, which means that separating your work life from your personal life is going to be a challenge. But it's even worse than that, because the small business you own is you.

After I quit my job, I had the horrifying realization that despite having no experience at all in my new job (Famous Celebrity Trans Person), I was not going to receive any training for it whatsoever. Not only would I not receive any training for it at the beginning, but as it went on, I was never going to get a single performance review. The only people who would offer critiques of my job performance would either (a) have no idea what they were talking about (random strangers), or (b) be people who I employed.

There was another moment, in December of 2022, a year after this had all started, that stands out for me. In the spring I had hired a personal assistant. There was still a part of my brain that was shocked by this, to have some-one help me with things I could do perfectly well on my own. But in any case, I'd hired her, and that December I suddenly realized I might have a responsibility I hadn't thought of. A friend of mine had worked as a personal assistant before, and one afternoon I texted her to ask whether I should be giving my assistant a holiday bonus. She said that I should, and even though it was just a text message, I could feel her eye roll and the implied "of course" that she didn't type.

While I had envisioned many possible outcomes for my life, including fame and riches, one possibility I had never planned for was that I might become an employer. But now I was. I was my assistant's boss. If it came down to it, if I didn't give her a holiday bonus, which she deserved, or otherwise failed to treat her well, she'd have every right to leave and go find a different employer who would place an appropriate value on her service. I would have done the same thing, as any employee ought to if they can. When you own the business, you can't quit. And it feels strange to know that everyone you employ can never be as dedicated to your company's success, your own success, as you are. And they shouldn't be. You chose to start this business; you can't blame anyone else for its success or failure.

The other thing you can't do is complain. Even now, I feel reluctant to be talking about the downsides of fame because I love it and do feel incredibly lucky. I used to be a software engineer working in the Silicon Valley tech industry. But for the most part, my social circle didn't have any other tech people in it. My friends were aspiring actors or stand-ups or writers; or else they were activists, or working for nonprofits. And yet, we all had jobs. We worked for an outside entity, and as such we all had certain complaints and joys and doubts and hopes in common. But when I became famous, suddenly it became so much harder to hang out and complain about my job with my friends.

My three or four closest friends were still always open to hearing how I felt. But I could also always feel their unspoken (and occasionally spoken) inability to take my problems seriously. I was a millionaire. I had become one of "those people"; I had hit the jackpot; I had a level of financial security. What did I have to complain about?

And again: fair point! I wouldn't trade my life for anyone's, more or less. So how could I complain? Easy: the same way everybody can complain, all the time. The only difference is the amount of sympathy those complaints can draw out.

The same applies to you, dear reader. I'm not asking for your sympathy. But I've learned this: all those famous people who have written TV shows and movies and books about the experience of fame? They did a good job! All the clichés you see are true. It's wonderful, exhilarating, addictive. That's something I couldn't know without experiencing it, the addictive nature of fame. You see those celebrities who can't give up the fame, people whose careers peaked thirty years ago, still going on celebrity editions of reality shows, desperate to hold on to some scrap of fame. While I hope I don't become that person, I now understand why people do it.

When you're famous, people care about your opinion. Like, all the time. Strangers, journalists, other famous people, your assistant, your social media followers. When you say something, they will all pay attention, and they'll have their opinions about it one way or another. When some random person with three hundred followers, the kind I used to be, spends an hour crafting a relevant, elegantly worded tweet on an issue of the day, they are rewarded with, maybe, ten to twenty reactions. Whereas if I type whatever is in my head, it'll be a headline on *Newsweek*. People will DM me about it. I may even get interview requests. It's extremely gratifying, and I have to work hard to remind myself that it might not last forever.

One of the most recent lessons I've learned is to let go of one of the things I kept telling myself when this all started. I never spelled it out, but it was something along the lines of "Remember, Amy, this is all fake. None of the praise you get is deserved; you just got lucky." But then in December 2022, I got a message from an old high school friend asking me to testify against Ohio House Bill 454, which would have barred doctors from providing gender-affirming health care to minors in the state.

I was in New York to attend the Out100 Gala, but

I flew to Columbus for the day and testified on behalf of young trans people. I told the Ohio assembly members that even though my life was going incredibly well, beyond my wildest dreams, all of it would mean nothing to me without hormone therapy. That gender-affirming medical care was literally lifesaving, and I encouraged them to make it more, not less, available.

At first I felt like a fraud being there. When I arrived, there were a ton of people there to testify, way more than they were going to be able to fit in. Many of them were parents of trans kids. And the people who had invited me there were the people doing the work on the ground in Ohio, in assembly members' offices and nonprofits. Me? I was just living in the Bay Area and being a celebrity and getting toasters sent to me, not facing many of the challenges they were. But when I expressed my hesitation to them, they said, "Listen, you can do things that we can't because you're famous. You can bring attention to this that we couldn't get any other way. There's a lot of different work that needs to be done in any movement, and yours is valuable too."

They were right. This window of celebrity has allowed me to be of service to my community, in ways I could not have predicted. Some are on a larger scale, like testifying at the Ohio assembly. And others may seem small, like the trans person I met who shared with me that their eighty-four-year-old grandfather had watched me on the show and something finally clicked with him and he understood the importance of using the right name for people, and the right pronouns. Things with my own family went relatively smoothly when I told them I was trans, but there were some bumps. And to know that I've been able to get some families past those painful interactions is really, really great.

So after testifying in Ohio, I headed to the airport and went back to New York, landing around two p.m. I went to the gala that night. It was a ridiculous, fancy event with loud music and goodie bags. The people I'd just met in Columbus, none of them were there. They were back in their homes, getting a night's sleep before waking up the next morning for another day of fighting against the odds to protect trans kids. I was getting my name engraved on a champagne flute while eating hors d'oeuvres. It was a strange day.

What I did to become famous was answer a bunch of trivia questions. I'm proud of how I did that, and I'm honored that people connected with me. It means so much to me that I helped out trans people whose family members hadn't seen a trans person before out in the world. And what I've come to realize is this: the testifying and the parties—they're part of the same job. It was my job to go to the party and be seen at it so people could imagine what it would be like to celebrate with minor celebrities. I was exhausted by the end of that day. But I'm good at powering through exhaustion, especially when it's to enjoy the pleasures of fame and to do the work of using that fame for good.

So what's it like to be famous? I don't know. I'm just hoping to stay famous long enough to find out. That's @Jeopardamy on all my socials, and don't forget to check out my podcast.

CHAPTER NINE

What Did You Win on *Jeopardy!*?

"Why did you once give up on your Jeopardy! *dreams?*
"How much money did you win?"
"What was the biggest prize you took away?"

My *Jeopardy!* run entered the history books on January 26, 2022. It appears in the archives as a forty-game streak, running from November 17, 2021, to January 26, 2022, with winnings of $1,382,800, plus $2,000 for the second-place finish in game 41. But for myself, none of those statistics are quite right: when it started, when it ended, what I won.

I could say that my *Jeopardy!* run started when I was five or six years old, on some night I don't even remember, the night that I first sat on the living room floor while my parents watched this revival of a quiz show they had liked called *Jeopardy!*, with a new host named Alex Trebek.

Or, of course, I could say that my run started when I first auditioned for the show, some fifteen years ago, and then auditioned again and again, year after year, until I made it.

But neither of those explanations truly captures the beginning of my *Jeopardy!* run. The childhood dream, that first audition, they were the beginning of something, yes, but that thing ended in 2017, when I realized I was trans. When I knew I could no longer deny my identity and had no choice but to live openly as a trans woman, I closed the door on my *Jeopardy!* dreams.

Not because *Jeopardy!* wouldn't have had me on; I believe they'd already had trans contestants, but even if they hadn't, I knew the *Jeopardy!* ethos, and I knew that if a smart-enough trans person came along, they wouldn't hesitate to invite them on the show. I closed the door because I believed then that I would never be comfortable enough with myself to go on national television, since at the time, even leaving my apartment felt absolutely frightening.

Eventually I realized that, while I still feared that my appearance, my clothes, my hair, and most of all my voice would be disliked, both by me and by the viewing public, that fear no longer outweighed the happiness I knew I would feel at realizing my lifelong dream. I decided I was going to start trying out again, and that's when my actual *Jeopardy!* run began.

The next time the online test came along, I registered for it, although that brought its own dilemma. Should I use the same email address I'd always used, the one that would be associated in their records with my old name? On the one hand, I had a feeling that someone who had gotten close to being on the show a few times would be more likely to be selected. On the other hand, not only did I not want to be associated with my old name, doing so would also "out" me as trans. Even though I knew that being trans was no obstacle to appearing on *Jeopardy!*, and might even be a slight advantage, that old fear still lived in me.

I knew that if I was actually to be invited on the show, it would become clear at some point that I was trans, and I was starting to feel a certain pride in my identity. I decided to use the old email, "outing" myself as trans to them. Then I let that doubt go and went back to reviewing lists of vice presidents, notable murder mystery authors, and Best Picture winners until the test came along.

When I got invited to the final round of auditions, I was excited but didn't get my hopes up too much. I'd been there before. For the most part, I felt ready to be seen: my hairline had been surgically filled in, I had quite a few outfits I actually liked wearing, and I'd gotten some confidence with wearing makeup (except for eyeliner, which even now intimidates me), but one problem remained: my voice.

Hormones can do a lot for trans women, but if you've already gone through puberty, there are some things they can't fix, and one of the big ones is your voice. I had gotten some vocal feminization training and could speak in a fairly passable feminine voice when I really concentrated on it. But I couldn't (and still can't) imagine using that voice all the time, every day for months or years until it became my natural speaking voice. To use that voice with my friends would feel fake, as if I wasn't really talking to them, but doing an impression for them, of a person they'd never met. While I didn't mind being a little fake at work, using it all day just seemed exhausting.

I kept my original voice, but I still hated it. Hated it. As I've said, I loved to sing as a child, but once my voice dropped in puberty, I pretty much stopped singing entirely unless I was completely alone. When I went to mass with my parents, I would sing the hymns, but so quietly as to be almost inaudible.

Years of co-hosting a podcast, before and after transition, had helped me be slightly more tolerant of my speaking voice, but that only meant I could hear it with a kind of numbed indifference. Every time I was addressed as "sir" on the phone, a wave of self-loathing would come over me, sometimes for minutes, sometimes for days. This is still somewhat true. (If you work in customer service someday, and you see that you are talking to someone named Amy, please don't call them sir, regardless of what their voice sounds like.) When I attended the "in-person" audition (in 2020 it was actually over Zoom), I used my "feminine" voice, and I resolved that if I got on the show itself, I would do the same.

After years of effort, the call came: I was going to be on *Jeopardy!* I was excited, of course, but still scared. The main fear was the one that had caused me to give up briefly, that fear of widespread hatred and scorn for being trans. I began practicing using my feminine voice for giving answers and planned out my first anecdote so I could practice the voice with that as well. As long as I used that voice, I told myself, maybe some people wouldn't even notice I was trans, and I might be spared the worst of the hate.

Due to various delays, my taping wound up getting pushed back by a year, and for nearly the entire time, I practiced my voice off and on and had every intention of using it on the show. Just a few days before my taping was scheduled to take place, I realized that I had changed in such a way that using that feminine voice not only no longer felt like the safe move, it felt deeply wrong.

For one, I had realized that being trans in public carried responsibilities. I knew that many other trans people shared my vocal dysphoria, and that they had most likely never seen a trans woman with a voice like ours on-screen in any sort of sympathetic light. I certainly hadn't, so to hide my voice began to feel like a betrayal of my community.

I think the biggest reason I changed my decision was that, in the year between the call and the taping, I had started dating Genevieve. And Genevieve loved me, loved my voice. That put a big dent in that lingering self-hatred. If somebody as amazing and beautiful and perfect as Genevieve could love this voice, maybe it wasn't entirely bad? I still struggled with the decision, and I didn't finally choose until the actual day of the taping, but once I did, I knew I'd made the right choice.

There I was, in September 2021, with Genevieve driving me to the airport to fly to LA. The anxiety had been building for days. My hatred for myself had weakened significantly, yes, but my fear of other people's opinions hadn't really changed. Would any of the *Jeopardy!* crew be weird about it? Would any of the other contestants misgender me? Would they object to my identity, or (almost as bad) ask me a bunch of uncomfortable questions about it? By now I had mostly made my peace with that fear. My new fear had nothing to do with my identity: How would I feel afterward?

While I thought I had a good chance of doing okay at the game, it was a simple matter of statistics. You see, *Jeopardy!* episodes are taped—usually on Mondays and Tuesdays between the months of July and May—about three months before they air. They tape five episodes on each day, which results in ten episodes completed during each week of taping. Only the champion of each episode moves on to the next taping—so they go through a lot of contestants in two days! This means that out of the ten people whose *Jeopardy!* journeys began that Tuesday, at least nine, and possibly all ten, would have their *Jeopardy!* run end that same day. It was likely, then, that when I left LA, I'd be leaving *Jeopardy!* behind forever. The dream that had started in half-formed thoughts as I played with He-Man action figures on the floor while my parents watched strangers answer questions on TV, that had been part of the armor that carried me through my childhood (*Maybe I'm getting bullied now, but I'm a super genius who will win on* Jeopardy! *someday*), that had been one of the few hopes I'd deemed precious enough to rescue from the collapsed heap of my old male identity . . . That dream, in all likelihood, was about to end.

Not only would it end, but its end would be seen by millions, an unknowable number of whom might use that moment to spout cruelties about my identity and appearance that I'd only barely been able to stop internalizing. After all that time, all I might get was thirty minutes of screen time, a few hundred bucks, and a smattering of insults on social media. I had worked hard to be okay with this, and I mostly was; after all, being on *Jeopardy!*, even for a single episode, is really cool! But I still felt a dread that this trip would be an anticlimactic end to a lifetime of effort.

Of course, as you already know, it wasn't! I defeated an impressive champion (with a bit of Final *Jeopardy!* luck), then won some more games, and then some more, and it became clear my run would last well beyond that Tuesday. But when did it actually end?

You could say that it ended on November 9, 2021, the day we taped the episode in which librarian Rhone Talsma ended my forty-game streak (with a bold Daily Double wager and a bit of Final *Jeopardy!* luck of his own). Yet at that point, as far as the world knew, my run hadn't even started.

You could say my run ended when my last episode aired on January 26, 2022, but that doesn't seem right either. There was still the Tournament of Champions to come, of course, and given the success I'd had, it seemed probable that there would be even more *Jeopardy!* in my future after that. But even if you set that aside, my run as "Amy Schneider, *Jeopardy!* champion" is still ongoing, and probably always will be. For the rest of my life, I will forever be associated with the events of those few months, and it seems fair to say that my *Jeopardy!* run will never end.

I don't want to discount the monetary reward: a million dollars is a jaw-dropping amount of money to win by answering trivia questions, and for me and Genevieve (and Meep and Rue, the two most beautiful cats in the whole world), that alone changed the course of our lives. But it's really only the beginning of what I've gained from this experience.

I've gotten to reconnect with all sorts of people from my past: old friends, teachers, castmates from long-ago productions of *Twelfth Night* and *The Lion in Winter*. I've been on the big screen at a Warriors game and heard applause from an entire arena. I've gotten to appear on *Good Morning America*, talk to journalists I admire, have my picture in the *Washington Post* and the *New York Times*. My work was published on my favorite website. I've gotten to spend time with the *Jeopardy!* crew, who were uniformly amazing people doing incredible work, and who I can't wait to meet again when the time comes. I've had all sorts of people and companies send me gifts, from chocolate chip cookies to designer clothing, and been recognized by the GLAAD Media Awards—all just for being myself on TV. And, of course, I got the opportunity to talk to you, through this book.

Before any of that, I got an even bigger prize. Until I appeared on television, I did not believe that the world would ever accept me for who I was. I had come to believe, not without some difficulty, that at least some people accepted me. But I still believed that those people were the exceptions, and that most people would see the things that I'd been raised to see in people like me: a freak, mentally ill, silly at best and evil at worst.

So as the days counted down to my episodes airing, I braced myself. Rejection was sure to come. And then . . . it didn't.

Sure, a few isolated voices popped up here and there to spew their hatred, but the overwhelming reaction was one of support and acceptance. It turns out most people simply believe me when I say who I am! They accept me as I am, with my stubble, my voice, my thin hair. They don't think there's something wrong with me. Because of that, for maybe the first time in my life, I started to think there wasn't anything wrong with me either.

I also know that my public acceptance isn't due to any special qualities in myself, or at least those qualities aren't the most important reason for it. The acceptance I've received is the fruit of long, violent struggles—some famous, some forgotten—in which trans people have risked their lives to secure their basic right to exist. Frances Thompson and Billy Tipton, Lili Elbe and Dora Richter, Sylvia Rivera and Felicia Elizondo, Laverne Cox and Gavin Grimm, and countless others have devoted themselves to creating the conditions that exist today, where a trans *Jeopardy!* champion can be, for most people, uncritically accepted and celebrated as the person she is.

The biggest prize that I received from my *Jeopardy!* run is the ability to say that I, too, have helped that cause. I haven't thrown rocks at the police in protest or fought for my rights in the Supreme Court; all I really did was chase a lifelong dream of appearing on *Jeopardy!* and then answer a bunch of trivia questions. But I knew that I would be taking on that burden of representation, and I will always and forever be proud to say that I've done my little part, helped ease the path for future generations of trans people to live free, open, and happy lives. That feeling is worth far more to me than any monetary prize, any media attention, any free toasters. It's something I will cherish forever.

But I'm still keeping the million dollars. As I once said to Ken Jennings, I like money!

My parting advice to all you young readers, though, is this: it's really important to do two things, and one of them is to be proud of your identity, to own your identity, and to accept your identity; and the other thing is to not let that define you. The great things about you are the same things that are great about anybody: whatever they are—your intelligence, your kindness, your courage— that's who you are, just as much as any other part of your identity, and you deserve to be celebrated for all those things.

Jeopardy! Trivia

1. Who created the show *Jeopardy!*?

Julann Griffin and her husband, Merv Griffin

2. What did Julann and Merv Griffin originally plan to call the show that became *Jeopardy!*?

What's the Question?

3. What is the song that plays during Final *Jeopardy!*?

The song is "Think!," a lullaby that Merv Griffin wrote for his young son. He originally titled it "A Time for Tony."

4. How many people watch *Jeopardy!* per week?

27 million viewers

5. What is the name of the fan-built database of more than 500,000 *Jeopardy!* clues?

The J! Archive

6. What happens when all contestants have either zero or negative dollars at the end of Double *Jeopardy!*?

Final *Jeopardy!* is not played when this happens.

7. What does a contestant have to wait for before they hit their buzzer?

The light that signals that the host has finished reading the clue

8. What is the lowest score to date in *Jeopardy!* history?

–$7,400

9. What is the least amount of money a player will go home with?

$2,000. This is true even when players lose money (they don't have to pay back those negative numbers).

10. What was host of *Jeopardy!* for the longest amount of time?

Alex Trebek. Alex hosted more than 8,200 episodes across thirty-seven seasons!

11. What is the term for when all three contestants get the answer wrong?

A triple stumper

12. What is the most common category on *Jeopardy!*?

"Before & After"

13. What triggers a tie-breaker clue?

Two or three players tying for first place after each contestant unveils their Final *Jeopardy!* response

14. What happens when all three contestants bet all their winnings in Final *Jeopardy!*, and all three get the answer wrong?

There is no winner.

15. What is the number of clues written for each season of *Jeopardy!*?

14,030

16. What is the special competition among six of *Jeopardy!*'s highest-ranked champions, who compete for a chance to win $500,000 and the Alex Trebek Trophy?

Jeopardy! Masters. Amy Schneider was a contestant on the first *Jeopardy! Masters*, which happened in 2023.

17. What is the *Jeopardy!* spinoff in which celebrities compete against one another on behalf of charities that will benefit from their winnings?

Celebrity Jeopardy! The show first aired in 1992.

18. What is the special two-week *Jeopardy!* competition that first aired in 1987 in which thirteen- to seventeen-year-olds compete against one another?

The Teen Tournament. There have been some seasons that did not run, for various reasons. In 2023, the show brought back previous teen champions for a High School Reunion Tournament.

19. What is the first test you have to take to begin qualifying as a *Jeopardy!* contestant?

The Anytime Test. It has fifty clues, and you have only fifteen seconds per clue to answer.

Acknowledgments

First of all, I have to thank my collaborator, Tanya Lee Stone, for finding a version of my story that I didn't even know was in there. I also want to thank Celia Lee, my amazing editor, for shepherding this book along and putting up with my habitual procrastination with a never-failing cheerfulness. And I wouldn't have met either of them had it not been for my agent, Cait Hoyt, who brought all of us together. And to all of the many other people whose work went into the creation of this book, many of whom I have never even met, I offer my sincere gratitude.

There are many people in my life without whose support I would never have been in a position to write a book or have been capable of doing so when the opportunity came along. I have thanked them already in the adult version of this book, so I won't repeat all their names here, but I am still so appreciative of all they've done for me.

I'd especially like to thank all the teachers in my life, both those I named in the book and many others whom I could have named just as well. I'm grateful that I was given so much encouragement in my life to nurture and explore my curiosity. A good teacher is a gift that keeps rewarding you for the rest of your life.

And while I did already thank them in my adult book, I do want to thank Meep and Rue again, because they are the cutest cats in the whole world and deserve all the thanks and pats and treats that they can get.